THE POLITICS OF LIBERATION

THE POLITICS OF LIBERATION

JOHN M. SWOMLEY, JR.

LIBRARY
BRYAN COLLEGE
DAYTON, TN 37321

BRETHREN PRESS
Elgin, Illinois

104837

The Politics of Liberation

Copyright © 1984 Brethren Press, Elgin, Illinois

All rights reserved. No part of this book may be reproduced in any form without written permission from the publisher, except by a reviewer who wishes to quote brief passages in connection with a review in a magazine or newspaper.

Scripture quotations are from the Revised Standard Version of the Bible, copyrighted 1946, 1952 © 1971, 1973 by the Division of Education and Ministry of the National Council of the Churches of Christ in America and are used by permission.

Brethren Press, 1451 Dundee Avenue, Elgin, IL 60120

Cover design by VISTA III

Edited by Leslie R. Keylock

Library of Congress Cataloging in Publication Data

Swomley, John M., 1915-
    The politics of liberation.

    Includes bibliographies and index.
    1. Liberty. 2. Political science. 3. Power (Social sciences)
4. National liberation movements. I. Title.
JC571.S98   1984   320.2   84-14466
ISBN 0-87178-712-1

Printed in the United States of America

Contents

PREFACE

The drama of social change on our planet since World War II is indebted to various liberation movements. These include those of Gandhi against colonialism, Martin Luther King against racism, and those in Latin America against political and economic exploitation.

The word "liberation" has meaning only because of the widespread economic, military, and political oppression of millions of people throughout the world. It is this oppression that has given rise to theologies of liberation in Latin America and, more recently, those that undergird black liberation and women's liberation.

The primary problem is not the fact that there are oppressors and the oppressed; it is that there are entrenched systems of oppression that continue to function long after the immediate oppressors die or are killed. Liberation then means the destruction or the transformation of systems such as those that maintain the arms race, imperialism, racism, sexism, and monopoly capitalism. These systems cannot be made tolerable. They require drastic but nonviolent change.

This focus on social and systemic change is at the heart of the theological method the theologians of liberation use. Jon Sobrino, a European Jesuit working in Central America, points to the difference between the European and Latin American ways of doing theology. European theologians are basically concerned with rational explanation of the world. Immanuel Kant, who liberated reason from authoritarianism and established the autonomy of reason, symbolizes their approach. The Latin American theologians of liberation, however, view the task of theology as transforming, rather than merely explaining, the world. Karl Marx, who wrote, "The philosophers have only interpreted the world in various ways; the point, however, is to change it," symbolizes this approach.

In effect, European theology tries to demonstrate that the terrible poverty and injustice in the world does not destroy a meaningful belief in God. Liberation theology, however, insists that a meaningful belief in God requires changing the structures or systems of society that cause poverty. This leads them to the social sciences for help in analyzing the structures of society, in the same way that European theologians turn to philosophy for help in explaining the world.

Although numerous books have been written about liberation theology, little has been written about liberation and political theory. What is the relation of politics to liberation? What theories of government and political power fulfill the expectation of liberation movements? How shall we understand ideology and its contribution to these movements? This book will examine the meaning of a politics of liberation, Hebrew and Christian theories of government, and modern concepts of political realism and idealism. It will also discuss the relation of power and ideology to liberation and the roots of liberation in secular and biblical thought.

1

THE POLITICS OF LIBERATION

The important decisions of our time are political. It is these decisions that determine whether there will be peace or war, freedom or totalitarianism, racial equality or discrimination, food or famine. When there is drought in India or Africa, or when the officers of corporations and governments make decisions that cause suffering for millions of people, there are no remedies except political ones. Individual or group charity does not deal with the widespread hurt of political refugees, millions of children suffering from malnutrition, or whole peoples subjected to economic exploitation. The answer to such oppression is not aspirin to relieve pain or Band-Aids for wounds, but human liberation, and that involves political action.

But what is politics? We have suffered so long from stereotypes that we need to create a new understanding of politics. Modern conceptions of politics are frequently based on the idea that persons at the top with power to manipulate or control the people make policy. Many people view politics as bargaining or deals between politicians, generally at the expense of lower and middle income groups. They may even define politics as "the art of compromise," as if to imply that principle must always or usually be sacrificed in the interest of expediency. Probably a large majority of people think of politics solely in electoral terms, with competing candidates engaging in promises they won't fulfill and making assertions they can't support. Sidney Hillman, a labor leader during the Franklin Roosevelt era, defined politics in his *Political Primer for all Americans* as "the science of who gets what, when, and why." Politics is almost invariably associated with the acquiring of power or influence in government. Many assume that election or appointment to office carries with it the ability to influence the course of events. They tend to think of political power as identical with a position that entitles a person to direct or rule other human beings.

None of these interpretations is adequate. They merely describe one form of politics that is associated with dominating or ruling over people. There is a politics that is not concerned with achieving or maintaining governmental power and that does not involve itself in deals with or concessions to special interests at the expense of the people. Such politics is concerned with sharing power with others rather than taking power over others. It is primarily a politics of liberation, in that it is concerned with activity and organization that seeks to set persons free from whatever it is that demeans or oppresses them.

Anyone functions politically who acts to liberate human beings anywhere in the world, or who analyzes existing social structures in order to transform them. The most striking examples of such political activity are Moses, Jesus, Marx, and Gandhi, none of whom sought governmental authority or power over people. Yet they and the movements they launched have directly and decisively affected the course of human history.

Martin Luther King, who practiced a politics of liberation, saw no necessity of achieving a position in government or engaging in bargaining or compromise with those who hold such positions. He said:

> I have come to think of my role as one which operates outside the realm of partisan politics, raising the issues and through actions creating the situation which forces whatever party is in power to act creatively and constructively in response to the dramatic presentation of these issues on the public scene.[1]

Movements that are organized to seek freedom or justice or human dignity are political by their very nature, even if those movements or their leaders never seek control over any community or government. Such movements understand politics as the organization of power to secure bread and dignity for those in need of both. They also understand politics as more than the organization of power. There is a community of dispossessed in which respect for others who are poor or black or powerless is evident. The ancient Greek concept that politics is concerned with the welfare of the city (polis) is transformed into a concern for the welfare of the community of the powerless. There is a sense in which most of us feel powerless to influence the events that control our lives. The poor either tend to identify themselves with those who are rich or glamorous or powerful, or else they resign themselves to their lot. Members of the middle class identify themselves with the economic, political, and military systems that keep them from any control over their own destiny. For these systems largely predetermine an arms race; preparation for nuclear war; inflation; pollution of the air, water, and land; organized crime; and senseless violence and vandalism. Those who make up the middle class support the military system on the assumption that there is no alternative to national preparation for eventual war, even though a nuclear war would destroy them, their children, and their property. They support economic and political systems in order to have a standard of living that gives them merely some power over the kind of house and car they own or the college to which they send their children. Though they would be surprised at the idea and unable to admit it, they are nearly as powerless as the poor. This means that the art of communicating to the general population the need for their own liberation is a political task.

Politics at its best is radical, in that it deals with the roots of human problems. It is also multidimensional in its recognition that there may be many causes and more than one solution to the problem of oppression. A politics of liberation is built in part on a recognition that all of us are creatures of our past, including the oppressive structures of history. Every black American has to acknowledge his/her inheritance of slavery, segregation, and the psychological attitude of loss of self-worth that these created. Likewise, white America must acknowledge its slave-master past, its role as an oppressor and robber of human dignity. Frantz Fanon cited cases of Algerians and Europeans who had clear symptoms of mental disorders as a result of violence of various types in which they or people close to them engaged. He wrote, "In other words, we are forever pursued by our actions. Their ordering, their circumstance and their motivation may perfectly well come to be modified *a posteriori*. This is merely one of the snares that history and its various influences sets for us."[2]

Politics, like religion, has its "original sin" with which we must deal before we can be free. To be liberated we must acknowledge our inheritance, accept it with sorrow rather than bitterness, and determine to change it. This means acknowledging our current involvement in oppressive systems and the fact that we continue to be shaped by them. At the same time we know that our human ancestors created the various systems under which we live, such as war, monopoly capitalism, imperialism, and racial segregation. We know that human beings can eliminate or transform them in this or succeeding generations. In the light of this knowledge, political as well as religious sin is collaboration with these systems to keep people in a state of bondage or exploitation. Sin is "the acceptance or willing of such unfreedom."

Sin is therefore related to powerlessness in that we resign ourselves to our seeming inability to transform the systems that are so harmful to people, not only in the Third World or in the black ghetto but everywhere. We know what these systems do to people, and yet we feel caught in them. Most of us are unprepared politically or emotionally to engage in defiance of even one of these systems. Liberation therefore begins with the ending of our bondage to powerlessness so that we experience freedom ourselves and have faith that collectively with other persons we can actually be instruments of political change.

Those who engage in a politics of liberation must have a consciousness, also found in mature religion, that no one can be saved or liberated alone. A black person or a Native American cannot be liberated as an individual so long as the majority of white Americans have stereotyped feelings about blacks or Indians as a group. No pacifist can experience liberation from war while his neighbor's son is militarized and his brothers and sisters overseas are being bombed. A black football star may be accepted without discrimination in housing and various other social relationships in the city that is the home of his professional team, but experience the treatment generally accorded all other blacks when he travels to Michigan, Missouri, or Arkansas. Until all blacks are liberated, there is a sense in which no one is. Nor are black people likely to be free unless a significant number of white Americans are also liberated from their separation and prejudice.

A politics of liberation is most easily understood by contrasting it with a politics of domination. Domination or power over people is evident in all efforts to control or manipulate people in the interest of a race, class, party, or some other elite group. Such control is not simply the product of wilful or evil persons, but is usually embodied in social structures or systems that benefit some groups more than others. The profits and privileges of the war system are evident in the Pentagon and the offices and business interests associated with the military-industrial complex. The capitalist system operates in the interest of large multinational corporations and those who are wealthy, just as the Soviet system provides more power and privileges to the upper levels of the Communist Party.

Social structures are built and maintained by ideology or the power to impose ideas on the people. They are also maintained by the financial manipulation of those who are economically dependent on the system to survive. They are maintained by still other forms of power that are punitive in nature, such as the power to imprison, threaten, or use violence against those who would change the system.

A politics of liberation, however, is concerned with empowering people rather than controlling them, with meeting their needs rather than exploiting them. It must necessarily be concerned with transforming the social structures that oppress people. It must also oppose the whole ideology of domination that makes the structures of oppression acceptable to many of those who suffer most from them. Many of the oppressed are not opposed to domination as such, but merely to being oppressed themselves. They tolerate exploitation, degradation, and humiliation because of a hope that they or their children may move into a position where they can enjoy the benefits of wealth or power or command. Or perhaps they feel powerless to change conditions. As Alan Boesak wrote with respect to blacks in South Africa, "the strongest ally of the oppressor is the mind of the oppressed."

Self-respect and the realization that each of us has power are important political resources. When the oppressed realize that those in power are at least as dependent on them as they are on the rich and powerful, they can overcome their submissiveness. Something tantamount to a religious conversion is essential to convince those with little self-respect and no obvious power that they are important and can reject or resist the structures that degrade them.

Probably the most dramatic statement setting forth a rejection of the politics of domination was that made by Jesus to his followers: "You know that those who are supposed to rule over the Gentiles lord it over them, and their great men exercise authority over them. But it shall not be so among you; for whoever would be great among you must be your servant."[4]

Gandhi is probably the best known person in modern times who practiced a politics of liberation based on servanthood and the renunciation of government position. Chester Bowles reports an incident that is typical of Gandhi's whole approach to politics:

> Gandhi was distressed to find the Indian National Congress largely a party of the educated and wellborn. It had almost no roots in the villages, and indeed no program except the goal of self-government, Swaraj, which was to be achieved by the usual kind of liberal agitation, parading, and petitioning. "The contrast between the palaces of New Delhi and the miserable hovels of the poor laboring class nearby cannot last one day in a free India, in which the poor will enjoy the same power as the richest in the land," Gandhi warned the Congress.
>
> On his first visit to an annual Congress session, he had found the camp's latrines uncared for. When fellow Congress workers told him this was the outcast's or untouchable's work, he found a broom and did the cleaning himself.
>
> The revolution which he proposed had to begin first in the life of the revolutionary. The voluntary acceptance of austerity and disciplined village service by the creative, educated people would combine with the power of the awakening peasants and workers. Out of this association would come a democratic and peaceful revolution that would achieve Ramaraj as well as Swaraj; that is, good government as well as self-government.[5]

The emphasis on serving and meeting the needs of others that is characteristic of a politics of liberation almost always involves a renunciation of governmental as well as economic power. This is not a philosophy of anarchy but a recognition that it is difficult, if not impossible, to identify with the oppressed while occupying a position of power over them. It may be technically possible for a person who identified with the poor and powerless to serve a term in Congress, although it would be difficult to get adequate campaign funds except from those who are affluent. But once in Congress a person would find it even more difficult to represent the oppressed on all issues and still be reelected. The whole system of oppression in the United Staes is related to certain structures. Taxation has loopholes for the upper classes. Military appropriations feed the military-industrial complex and manage the monopoly capitalist system. The F.B.I., C.I.A., and other federally aided police programs have focused more on radicals who would change the system than on criminals who act illegally within it. Vigorous day-after-day opposition to these and other crucial aspects of our existing system of oppression is probably impossible for any elected official. Yet only such consistent activity would maintain identification with the powerless people of society.

It is certainly true that if anyone aspires to be an official of the United States or any other government, he or she must act as such officials are expected to act. One cannot be President of the United States without accepting the responsibilities that the capitalist economic system, the military system, and other structures of our society at present impose upon elected and appointed officials.

Much of government operates in secrecy, with confidential briefing of members of Congress by civilian and military officials. It is difficult to discover what takes place and who bribes whom with one favor or another. The theory of Jefferson, Madison, and others of the American Founding Fathers was that free discussion was the only way to preserve and strengthen society. A wise national policy, they believed, necessarily depended on free public discussion, searching criticism of proposed policies, and assurance that truth had power. However, in contemporary America elected officials who reveal official secrets or even the opinions given in briefings are viewed as betrayers of government, because government is identified with rule by dominant interests who do not want to share information or power.

There is a fundamental contradiction between a politics of

liberation and a politics of domination. Those who seek liberation cannot be effective by accepting roles or methods that presuppose the subordination of one group of people to another. When whole sections of the population are denied information because they are viewed as potential adversaries of the prevailing policy, there can be neither democratic discussion nor the sharing of power.

Liberation is based on the idea of respect for persons, including opponents and enemies. If a liberated community is one where each person and his opinions are respected by all, then the process of liberation begins now with respect for the personhood of everyone. There is a clear connection between the way we treat persons now and the way we want society to be organized.

The early Christian approach to politics was based on both this idea of respect and concern for everyone, and a nongovernmental stance. During the first two centuries A.D., Christians abstained from seeking any office that would would give them power over other people. They took seriously Jesus' idea that they were to serve rather than rule. They formed communities of liberation in an age and empire in which oppression was taken for granted. These communities made no distinction between those who were slave or free, male or female, Hebrew, Greek, or barbarian. There was no participation in such major structures of oppression as war or the administration of the imperial or governmental systems. Some of these communities even held material possessions in common for the benefit of all. Their primary allegiance was to the new community, although they were asked to obey the laws of the Roman Empire insofar as they did not conflict with the demands of the new community.

The political thought of the early Christians differed from that of the Greeks, who gave us the word *politics*. Politics in ancient Greece, as we have already noted, was a term related to the welfare of the city (*polis*). In practice, however, the city was founded on human slavery, so that the welfare of the city related primarily to those who were already free citizens. The Christian concern was the for welfare of the new community drawn from all nations and economic and social groups, rather than the welfare of a geographic city or those who were freeborn.

The early Christian approach is a prototype of a liberated community in its respect for everyone, its classless organization of the community, and its renunciation of governmental power over other human beings. It can, of course, be argued that the unwillingness of the early Christians to support war and governmental administration was withdrawal from politics. On the other hand, the withdrawal of support, known today as civil disobedience, can be a very powerful political weapon. Civil disobedience is not simply the deliberate and nonviolent refusal to obey an unjust law. It can also be the refusal to support a regime or system that is illegitimate because it oppresses rather than serves the people. Such refusal has brought about the fall of governments in Guatemala, Chile, El Salvador and other nations.[6] The early Christians unknowingly exercised power by the very process of the renunciation of power or, in other words, withdrawing consent from the most oppressive aspects of Roman rule. That withdrawal of consent was not based solely on their opposition to oppression evident in the empire, but on their loyalty to their own new organization of society. They believed that their own community should embody the kind of human relationships that would exist in a future society in which God's will was fully practiced.

A politics of liberation today likewise looks forward to a liberated community. No blueprint exists for such a community. However, a community could not be said to be liberated if it supported racial segregation, extremes of poverty and wealth, war, or any structured superiority and inferiority. A liberated society is not a classless society in the sense of complete equality, for in any complex social order some persons will be in positions in which they make administrative or other decisions that affect the work of others.

An obvious task for those seeking liberation is to devise ways to prevent or minimize the control by an elite of the economic and political life of a community. It is to create institutions or structures through which the people can control, discipline, or recall administrators who begin to dominate or disable or demean those whose work they direct. The devising of such structures, however, would not guarantee their use. That is one reason the concern of a politics of liberation is not with blueprints of the future but with creating a consciousness of liberation.

A politics of liberation necessarily has a theory of government, but it does not begin with efforts to restructure federal or state governments. It begins with the social, economic, and political units on which our existence as persons depends. These include such groups as the family, the school, labor unions, farm and professional associations, the churches, organizations for peace or racial equality, women's movements and other voluntary associations, and eventually villages, towns, and municipalities. Unless these express the spirit of liberation by eliminating their own manifestations of oppression, their own exclusiveness and support of disabling systems, there is not likely to be fundamental change at state and national levels. Politicans in Washington, even today, seldom rise much above or sink much below the level of public opinion.

Liberation also means freedom to choose wider loyalties than those into which one has been born or reared. However, there can be no freedom to enjoy cultural development and human fellowship in various social units unless basic economic needs are met. Liberation from poverty or economic scarcity is indispensable to true freedom because the complete absence of leisure necessarily means slavery to production. Liberation is also more than freedom from poverty. Unless workers are more than tools in the hands of management, they are not able to determine their own destiny. Workers must therefore be able to share in the control of industries and the economy as well as political power.

The fact that human beings cannot create a perfect society does not mean that liberation is a politically foolish concept. Specific oppressive structures that human beings have created can be altered, transformed, or eliminated by this and subsequent generations.

What is important now is to develop a consciousness of liberation, a new way of thinking politically. That new way of thinking begins with a renunciation of power over people. It involves the organization of movements whose goal is liberation, rather than the acquiring of governmental power for themselves. It necessarily involves serving the people who are oppressed. There is a difference between service and subservience. A serving community meets its needs and those of others who are oppressed. It is powerful because of its human solidarity, its self-reliance and human dignity. Even though oppressed, it is conscious of its own strength and worth. A subservient group, on the contrary, is generally disorganized. Its self-image is one of little worth. It tends to ask favors and offer its support to those who are more likely to provide the most crumbs from their bounty. One task of a politics of liberation is to help subservient groups become serving communities.

The concept of a liberated and serving community is not simply the product of Utopian thinking. It grows out of our human nature, which requires freedom both for maximum development and for the exercise of responsibility. It is similarly rooted in the theological assumption that human beings are not puppets manipulated by some deity but are free to make their own choices in a world that is friendly to cooperation, community, and human responsibility. It also grows out of a concept of government whose origin and nature are the subject of the following chapter.

THE ORIGIN AND NATURE
OF GOVERNMENT

Liberation ought to be the goal of good government. In practice government has seldom been liberating to all of its citizens. Instead it is largely a record of rule by a dominant group. Many political scientists and theologians would even indicate that government originated in the necessity to curb aggressive individuals or groups and must steadily maintain an upper hand.

All of the major theories of the origin of government find expression in the experience of the Hebrew people. Unlike other theories of government, such as the one expressed in Plato's *Republic*, there is no one developed approach to government in the Hebrew Scriptures because these writings are primarily experiential rather than theoretical.

Aside from the varieties of Hebrew experience with government, the virtue of discussing Hebrew literature as political theory is its unique emphasis on liberation as the basis for good government. This too is rooted in experience, as ancient Israel traced its origins to a group of liberated slaves who accepted leadership but not dominance.

No one can state precisely how government originated. There are, however, a number of major theories about its origin that shed light on the meaning and nature of politics. One explanation is that a group of people got together to subdue or dominate another group of people by force and violence. The fact of slavery in the ancient world makes it easy to believe that government began with an initial seizure of power by an aggressive group. Franz Oppenheimer states this position as follows: "The moment when first the conqueror spared his victim in order to exploit him in productive work was of incomparable historical importance. It gave birth to nation and state. . . ."[1]

There are passages in the Hebrew Scriptures or Old Testament that seem to confirm this view. Some describe the complete slaughter of an entire people (2 Chronicles 20:23f.), whereas others indicate that under certain circumstances the right thing to do is to take people captive rather than to slay them (Deuteronomy 20:10-15). This idea, that government began with a dominant group, finds modern expression in the idea that the state is chiefly an instrument of the ruling class.

A second theory of the origin of government is called the social contract. The historical explanation of this theory is based on the assumption that at one time humans were without government and banded themselves together for protection or for other reasons.

The idea has its roots in the Hebrew idea of covenant. In Genesis 17:6-7 God said to Abraham, "I will make nations of you and kings shall come forth from you. And I will establish my covenant between me and you and your descendants after you. . . . "

The social contract was not simply one between the people or the people and a ruler, but generally included God, so that it had an element of suprahuman authority and therefore of divine judgment when rulers exceeded their authority and became oppressors of the people.

The particular historical origin ascribed to the social contract theory is not essential to the theory and is even beside the point. The essential point is that governors and governments have a continuing legitimacy only through the consent of the people, whether or not there is any formal means of expressing that consent.

A third theory of the origin of government is that it is a product of history, probably rooted in the family and a gradual development through various extensions of the family into clans, tribes, and more complex forms. Robert MacIver in his *Web of Government* wrote:

> To ascribe the beginning of government to force or to contract or to some particular conjuncture is to ignore the fact that already in the family, the primary social unit, there are always present the curbs and controls that constitute the essence of government. Government is not something that is invented by the cunning or the strong and imposed on the rest. Government,

however much exploitation of the weak by the strong it may historically exhibit, is much more fundamental than these explanations imply. It is the continuation by the more inclusive society of a process of regulation that is already highly developed in the family.[2]

According to this theory it is community and the authority of a community of people that is more basic to social organization than armed force. It is not necessary to cite specific references to show that this theory of government has well-developed roots in the Hebrew Scriptures. The tribes of Israel thought of themselves as an outgrowth of patriarchal families and even referred to God as the God of Abraham, Isaac, and Jacob. The word *Israel* is simply another name for the patriarch Jacob.

The chief biblical theory of the origin of government is that God ordered or created it. The Hebrew concept of the state was that of a theocracy in which the law of God and the law of government were identical. Human rulers were selected and anointed by God. Sometimes this was done directly, as when God called upon Moses to liberate the people of Israel from slavery in Egypt (Exodus 3:4f). Sometimes prophets were the spokesmen of God, as when Samuel said to Saul, "The Lord sent me to anoint you king over his people Israel. . . " (1 Samuel 15:1). The concept of the ruler being the instrument of God carried over into the New Testament so that Jesus at his trial is reported as saying to Pilate, "You would have no power over me unless it had been given you from above. . . " (John 19:11).

Luther suggested that there are orders of creation or institutions that were ordained by God in the sense that they were apparently present from the very beginning. All children owe their birth to one man and one woman, and their nurture to all those in the family.

Some kind of governing authority and economic system were also present from the beginning. This is a biblical view that the apostle Paul also asserted: "There is no authority except from God, and those that exist have been instituted by God" (Romans 13:1). This is a different concept of government from that of the Greeks, who believed government had its origin in the political nature of human beings.

The biblical emphasis on the divine origin of authority is not to be interpreted as an endorsement of a particular government or political organization. The modern nation-state, which came into being in 1648 following the Reformation and the religious wars, is not an order of creation but a development or contingency of history, as was the Holy Roman Empire and its predecessor, the Roman Empire.

In both the Hebrew and the Christian Scriptures particular forms of government or specific rulers are not understood as divinely ordained in the sense that they are perfect agents of God's will. When the people of Israel wanted a king to rule over them, Samuel described the oppression that would inevitably accompany the reign of an earthly king, including the taking of "your fields and vineyards," a "tenth of your seed," as well as "your sons" and "your daughters" to serve him (1 Samuel 8:10-17). The prophets also pointed to the tyranny and evildoing of their own rulers and those in nearby lands. Jesus similarly had reservations about those in political authority. King Herod had beheaded John the Baptist and was reported to Jesus as wanting to kill him. Jesus described Herod as "that fox" (Mark 6:14-28; Luke 13:31f.). He also referred to an unjust judge (Luke 18:1-8) and warned his followers against the courts.

The biblical view of government is that it is of divine origin, a necessary agent of God to maintain order, but an imperfect instrument that often acts contrary to God's liberating purpose.

It is possible that each of these theories about the origin of government is helpful in understanding politics and government today. The biblical conception that government is an essential aspect of creation suggests its necessity and its contribution to human order. The idea that government evolved from the extended family indicates that government is not rooted in violence but in community. It also means that specific forms of government are the creation of different groups of persons. The social contract theory holds that governments have no right to exist unless they have the continuing support of the people. The theory that government began when one group decided to dominate another has validity only insofar as it expresses the fact that modern government with few exceptions operates in the interest of the ruling class. In capitalist countries this refers to the upper economic groups and the huge corporations that in the United States are frequently identified with the military-industrial complex. In the Soviet Union it is the party hierarchy, the upper levels of the bureaucracy, the military, and technologists who dominate.

These theories and the usual view, both in our contemporary world and in history, hold that those who rule and govern—kings, presidents, and dictators— shape politics and the future. In the ancient world many empires traced their origin and authority to a king descended from heaven or the gods. Ancient Israel, however, is responsible for a unique theory of politics and government. It traced its origin to the liberation of a group of slaves. In those days it was not a king but Yahweh (God) who had liberated the slaves from their taskmasters in Egypt (Exodus3:7). His title was the Deliverer or the Liberator, the one who sets slaves free. He is reported as saying to Moses "I have seen the affliction of my people who are in Egypt, and have heard their cry because of their taskmaster: I know their sufferings, and I have come down to deliver them. . .(Exodus 3:7f.) The biblical account clearly shows that Yahweh was directing Moses through every step of the liberating process.

Moses brought about the first unified leadership of the tribes of Israel, but he held no official position, just as Gandhi had none. Moses' authority was great enough, however, that he was able to appoint his successor. But once the Israelites were settled in Canaan there was no central authority. Decentralized or local government by leaders emerged when circumstances called for it. The phrase "Every man did that which was right in his own eyes" (Judges 21:25) not only indicates the absence of central government, but also the importance attached to freedom.

The most probable interpretation of the main political thrust of the entire Bible is that it is against the kind of government exemplified by those who rule over their subjects and are therefore able to oppress them. Instead, typical rulers are viewed with suspicion, and government is judged by its promotion of freedom and the degree to which it serves the people.

An example of the early attitude toward the monarchy is found in the fable of Jotham, which comes out of the context of

Abimilech's making himself a king in Shechem:

> The trees went forth once to anoint a king over them; and they
> said unto the olive tree, 'Reign thou over us.' But the olive tree
> said unto them: 'Should I leave my fatness, wherewith by me
> they honour God and man, and go to be promoted over the
> trees?' And the trees said to the fig tree, 'Come you, and reign
> over us.' But the fig tree said to them, 'Shall I leave my sweetness
> and my good fruit, and go to sway over the trees?'
> Then said the trees unto the vine, 'Come you, and reign over us.'
> And the vine said unto them: 'Should I leave my wine, which
> cheereth God and man, and go to be promoted over the trees?'
> Then said the trees unto the bramble, 'Come you and reign over
> us.' And the bramble said unto the trees: 'If in truth you anoint
> me king over you, then come and put your trust in my shadow;
> and if not, let fire come out of the bramble, and devour the
> cedars of Lebanon' (Judges 9:8-15).

This political satire likens the leadership of a king to the
shade that a thornbush lacks, and suggests that it may even
destroy the bushy cedar that provides the best shade. So the
king is viewed as someone who wants to control or dominate
others and therefore who would destroy freedom, the most
precious value they had. Later, after Abimelech was killed in
battle, Israel returned to a society without kings (Judges 10:1-5).

When Israel finally accepted Saul as its first monarch, it
was not without Samuel's advice to the contrary (1 Samuel
8:6-18). When the people said to Samuel, "Give us a king to
govern us", Samuel took the problem to Yahweh, who said:
"Hearken to the voice of the people in all that they say to you;
for they have not rejected you, but they have rejected me from
being king over them." Then Samuel was instructed to warn the
people of the dangers of having a king. These dangers included
taking their sons to war and their daughters as "perfumers,
cooks and bakers." The king would also take the best land, a
portion of the grain and grapes and "will take your menservants
and maidservants, and the best of your cattle and your asses and
put them to his work . . . and you shall be his slaves." The people, however, insisted: "We will have a king over us, that we
also may be like all the nations, and that our king may govern
us and go out before us and fight our battles (1 Samuel 8:19,20).

Israel turned to a king to defend itself from the growing threat of the Philistines.

The experience of the people with their early kings, Saul and David, was on the whole good. But David's son Solomon began to use forced labor (1 Kings 5:13). The result was a revolt that was suppressed. Rehoboam, Solomon's son, rejected the advice of a people's assembly "to lighten the hard labor of your father" and instead told them he would be even harsher than Solomon (1 Kings 12:3-11). The people's response to such a threat was "What portion have we in David . . . to your tents, O Israel" (1 Kings 12:16). So Israel was divided because its kings enslaved the people. Rehoboam was able to retain rule only over Judah. The other tribes to the north set up their own kingdom under Jereboam.

The conflict between the people and the king continued. The Israelites' freedom was evident in the account of the attempt by King Ahab to get the vineyard of Naboth, which bordered the king's property. The king offered another vineyard or its value in money. But Naboth said: "The Lord forbid that I should give you the inheritance of my fathers (1 Kings 21:3). The king, recognizing the traditional right of the Israelite to his land, went back home. But when the queen, a Phoenician who did not accept that traditional right, arranged the death of Naboth, there was an immediate criticism from Elijah the prophet, who asserted that Ahab's dynasty would be destroyed. Again and again other prophets such as Amos and Jeremiah indict the kings of Israel for not recognizing the freedom that Yahweh had given to the people.

The abuses of the monarch and the prophetic criticism of them led to a wholly new view of the king, which was incorporated in the Deuteronomic reformation. Functions that the king had earlier performed were taken away. Judges and officers were to be appointed in all the towns for the purpose of administering justice (Deuteronomy 16:18). Officers of militia were in charge of preparing for war, except that prior to a battle the priest would build up the morale of the fighting men (Deuteronomy 20:1-9). The prophetic function of speaking for God remained with the prophets (Deuteronomy 16:14-18). The king was instructed not to multiply horses—in other words, not to increase his chariots or his ability to make war

(Deuteronomy 17:16)—nor might he increase his wealth or the size of his harem. Instead he was to be the servant of God, one who read the law and kept all its words. He was to be chosen from among the brotherhood and be an example to the people so "that his heart may not be lifted up above his brethren . . . " (Deuteronomy 17:15, 18-20).

The Deuteronomic reformation proposed a separation of governmental powers with Yahweh as the head, who ruled through the law that the judges administered, the prophets interpreted, and the priests guarded and protected. The role of the king was that of a representative of the people, an ombudsman as well as a model Israelite. This restructuring of the king's functions by reducing and limiting his traditional sovereignty and elevating all of his fellow Israelites to the status of king's brothers was a revolutionary political concept.[3] In Psalm 72, which presumably celebrates the coronation of the king, the prayer suggests that the king was to deliver the poor and the needy and liberate their lives "from oppression and violence."

A more radical concept of the king is given in Isaiah. The true ruler is not merely a brother to his fellow Israelites, but a servant, one who takes the place of those who are arrested and punished by oppressors (Isaiah 53:8). "He was wounded for our transgressions, he was bruised for our iniquities" (Isaiah 53:5).

It was this concept of a servant and brother-king that motivated Jesus and stood at the heart of the idea of the kingdom of God on earth. Jesus clearly rejected the temptation to be like Caesar and rule the kingdoms of the world (Luke 4:5-8). He announced that the Spirit of the Lord had anointed him "to preach the gospel to the poor, deliverance to the captives . . . and to liberate those who are oppressed."

Jesus did not originate the term *Kingdom of God.* It was part of the popular longing, the messianic expectation that a kingdom of God would come to displace the kingdoms in which monarchs could and did function as tyrants. The kingdom of God did not refer to heaven or an afterlife but to a new era that would come on earth. Jesus also inherited the expression "eternal life." This was a common expression the people used to indicate that they wanted to live through the present age into the coming age when tyranny would be abolished.

The fact that each Israelite was originally a slave who had been set free was not only an incentive to political freedom from the monarch. It was also an argument for changed attitudes toward slavery as such. The book of Deuteronomy provides for the release of slaves every seven years (Deuteronomy 15:12, 13). It also provides that the slave is not to be sent away empty-handed; "You shall furnish him liberally from your flock, from your threshing floor, and from your winepress. . . ." The reason is this: "You shall remember that you were a slave in Egypt, and as Yahweh has blessed you, you shall give to him" (Deuteronomy 15:13-15). There was also provision for runaway slaves: "You shall not return to his master the slave who has escaped from his master to you; he shall dwell among you in the place that he shall choose . . . you shall not oppress him" (Deuteronomy 23:15f.). This expression of solidarity with the slave rather than with the master was not only more humane than the practice elsewhere in the ancient world, but it was also evidence of their heritage of liberation and predisposition toward it.

There were penalties for injuring or killing a slave (Exodus 21:20). One of them implied that a master who could not treat his slave humanely ought to set the slave free: When a man strikes the eye of his slave, male or female, and destroys it, he shall let the slave go free for the eye's sake (Exodus 21:26f.).

The idea of God as liberator is set forth in still another way in Leviticus 25, which tells of the year of jubilee. That is the fiftieth year, after seven times seven years. "And you shall hallow the fiftieth year and proclaim liberty throughout all the land unto all the inhabitants thereof . . . (Leviticus 25:10). It is a year when each person could reclaim ownership of his property that was sold for debt and each enslaved Israelite was to be set free. This year of jubilee had singular importance for Jesus, as John Howard Yoder suggests in *The Politics of Jesus.* The Lord's Prayer is a jubilee prayer. It includes the following petition: "Remit us our debts as we ourselves have also remitted them to our debtors." The year of jubilee is the "acceptable year of the Lord," which Jesus said he was called to preach (Luke 4:19).

The origin of Hebrew government in the liberation of slaves is not simply a fact of Hebrew history celebrated to this day in the Feast of the Passover. It is the starting point for a wholly different model of politics set forth in the Hebrew reaction to the monarchy and slavery. That model is one in which politics is the instrument of liberating change rather than simply a process for achieving and maintaining control over people. God was not a tyrant but a liberator. The prophets who spoke for God, such as Amos, Hosea, Isaiah, Jeremiah, and Micah, were not primarily concerned with denouncing occasional or specific acts of tyranny. They were opponents of the whole system. They spoke for all who were oppressed and against the privileged. They emphasized individual responsibility and righteousness as well as a restructured political community.

In summary, the Hebrew Scriptures claim that government is created by God, and government should reflect the purposes of God. God has liberated his people from slavery. Therefore they should free their slaves.

A second aspect of Hebrew political thought is that even in a theocracy in which God at least theoretically chooses and anoints the political leader, government does not always reflect the divine will. Kings and peoples are judged and found wanting. A frequent expression in the Scriptures describing the conduct of kings is "He did that which was evil in the sight of the Lord" (2 Kings 15:9). Because the kings and people went their own way and engaged in oppression, they were defeated in war and carried off into slavery.

A third aspect of Hebrew thinking is that God is freedom. Even though he preferred that Israel not be ruled by kings, he permitted the people to choose a form of government contrary to his will. The forms of government chosen over the years are therefore a product of human choice and do not necessarily reflect the divine purpose.

In the fourth place, there is a general recognition that governments and kings must be criticized. This is the function of the prophets. Governments must also be reformed and brought under control, as evident in the Deuteronomic reform. Here is the root of the idea that government, although instituted by God, is not necessarily to be obeyed and certainly not to be accepted without critical analysis. There is also evidence of civil disobedience in Daniel's continuing worship of God despite the king's degree forbidding it (Daniel 6).

The Hebrew Scriptures also accept the idea that the people

and individual Israelites have rights over against the government. This was evident in the conflict between Ahab the king
and Naboth (1 Kings 21).

Government was not deified or absolutized. It was always
measured or judged by its faithfulness to human freedom and
equal justice. In fact, the vision of good government and a good
king is that of a faithful servant of the people, especially a servant to those who are poor and oppressed.

CHRISTIAN THEORY OF GOVERNMENT

The fact that Christians are the largest religious group in the Western hemisphere, as well as in Europe and Africa south of the Sahara, raises questions about the future of a politics of liberation. Does Christianity have an adequate political theology to sustain the emphasis on liberation set forth by its parent, Judaism, or is it likely to continue a largely uncritical support of the major political, economic, and military systems?

Although many literal interpreters of the New Testament have claimed that Paul's statement in the thirteenth chapter of Romans is an endorsement of whatever government is in power, the Christian Scriptures begin with an attitude of suspicion toward government. That suspicion was obviously created by the conflict that had developed between Jesus and the Roman authorities, symbolized in the Crucifixion and in the martyrdom of many of his followers.

That conflict was set in the specific context of Roman imperialism. Jesus lived in a colony of the Roman Empire and therefore had to face the problem of both foreign political rule and Roman civil religion. Every Jew had to face the question whether he was for or against foreign rule, because the issue of imperialism had divided the nation. The Jewish power structure collaborated with Rome and had substantial support. Many Jews, however, wanted liberation from Roman control. One of their important arguments was a religious one—that no heathen ruler should receive the allegiance of God's people.

They were heirs of the Maccabean revolt but were more directly related to the tax-resistance movement of Judas of Galilee, a contemporary of Jesus' parents, Joseph and Mary. Judas Galilaeus had developed a political program that included liberation from Roman control by violent revolt. His program also asked loyal Jews to refuse to pay taxes to Rome and thereby stop financing the Roman army of occupation. His political and military headquarters had been established at Sepporis, three miles north of Nazareth. His revolt was crushed, but his martyrdom and the appeal of his message were not lost. According to Josephus, the Jewish sect or party known as the Zealots, which led the unsuccessful Jewish rebellion against the Romans in A.D. 66, was one of the results of the movement and martyrdom of Judas of Galilee. Alan Richardson demonstrates in the *The Political Christ* that the Zealot party was not in existence during Jesus' lifetime but was a later development.[1]

It is significant that Luke describes the birth of Jesus in the context of taxation: "And it came to pass in those days that there went out a decree from Caesar Augustus that all the world should be taxed" (Luke 2.1). Luke also reports, in the passage preceding this, that Zechariah in prophesying the birth of John the Baptist said that through him God had "raised up a horn of salvation for us in the house of his servant David . . . that he should be saved from our enemies and from the hand of all that hate us" (Luke 1:69, 71). When Luke wrote these words, and also when Jesus was born, the only real enemies of the Jewish people from whom they could be saved were the Romans.

In these passages Luke was obviously aware of the conflict between Jesus and Caesar and familiar with Israelite opposition to Roman rule. Matthew similarly used the political context and the conflict of Jesus with Caesar in his explanation of the birth of Jesus. That conflict was symbolized in the wise men's search for the King of the Jews and in the fact that Caesar's deputy, Herod, was troubled at the report about the wise men seeking out a new king who would "rule my people Israel" (Matthew 2:6). It was also symbolized in the story of Herod's desire to kill the newborn baby and the flight of Joseph, Mary, and Jesus into Egypt. The story quite plainly suggests that the wise men preferred to worship Jesus rather than pay homage to Caesar. When they returned home another way rather than report to Herod as he had asked, they had already decided against Caesar and for the new King.

Matthew continues the idea of conflict between Jesus and Caesar in the temptation experiences. Satan told Jesus he would give him all the kingdoms of this world—in other words, make him Caesar—if he would accept Satan's lordship and his methods. Jesus in this passage took for granted that Caesar was under Satan's control. When Jesus rejected the temptation, he also repudiated any idea of being like Caesar (Matthew 4:7-10).

Jesus also warned his disciples that they would "be dragged before governors and kings for my sake" (Matthew 10:18). This also suggested a conflict with Caesar.

The crucial passage for the interpretation of Jesus' attitude toward Caesar is probably the one in which the Pharisees who were tax resistant and the Herodians who supported taxes asked him about paying taxes to Caesar. The tax question was very important because of the economic problems of the people. Palestine year after year faced the possibility of famine. The population had reached the limits of the available food supply. The Roman governors taxed the people heavily and used the money for their own purposes. Frederick C. Grant refers to a Roman tax on land, a poll tax, a house tax, import and export taxes, a market tax, and a salt tax, as well as others. He writes, "At the lowest, the total taxation of Judea and Samaria in the time of Jesus must have approximated 25 per cent of all income; and very likely it was more—perhaps working up toward 35 or 40 percent."[2]

When Jesus' opponents asked him, "Is it right to pay the poll tax to the emperor or not," Jesus asked them for a denarius. Ethelbert Stauffer points out that this particular coin was the one used by the emperor to pay his officials, his soldiers, and his suppliers. When they received their pay, they could spend it for goods and services in the country they occupied. When the emperor wanted to do so, he would withdraw the coins from circulation and melt them into metal.[3] In this way the emperor's coins were used to pay the Roman army of occupation. When Jesus asked "Whose head and title is this?" on the coin, they responded "Caesar's." Stauffer indicates that their one-word reply was brief and grudgingly given because the inscription on the coin compromised the integrity of the Pharisees. The coin carried the head of Tiberius, with these words: "The August, the Image and Manifestation of the King of Heaven on Earth.[4] Jesus answered their question with the phrase "Render to Caesar what belongs to Caesar." The word "Render means "to give back." The coins were really Caesar's and were to be returned at his command. Jesus' own lack of possession of such a coin and his reply that the coin really belonged to Caesar was a rebuke to his questioners because they had the coin in their possession. They had accepted it in payment for something and therefore had "profited by the financial, economic and legal order of the empire."[5]

It is probable that many Jews did not have a denarius in their pockets. One of the early Christians, Hilary of Poitiers, wrote: "If we have nothing in our possession that belongs to Caesar, then are we free of the obligation of giving him what is his?"[6] Jesus' answer, then, implied tax exemption for those who did not have a denarius.

There is a further implication to this. Judaism taught that "taxes payable by Jews in the Holy Land were God's property . . . God's claim to the taxes rested upon his title to all material possessions."[7] For example, "The earth is the Lord's and the fullness thereof" (Psalm 24:1), or "All things come of thee, and of thine own have we given thee . . . "(1 Chronicles 29:14). Josephus wrote, "Now there is no public money among us except that which is God's."[8]

It was not only the heirs of Judas of Galilee but Pharisees—in other words, devout Jews—who felt they had no obligation to pay the tribute because everything belonged to God and tribute to a heathen ruler denied the sovereignty of God and their own sonship. So when Jesus added, "and render to God the things that are God's," he was speaking in the context of Jewish thought—that everything, including taxes, belong to God.

He had avoided their trap by verbally telling those who had Caesar's coin to give it back to him, but he did not thereby endorse paying taxes or giving anything else to Caesar. In the context of Jewish thought, he was saying that one's whole loyalty belonged to God, and nothing belonged to Caesar except a denarius with Caesar's head and title on it. "You shall love the Lord your God with all your heart, all your mind, and all your strength" left no room for a divided allegiance.

This interpretation of Jesus' attitude fits one of the accusations against Jesus at his trial before Pilate: "We found this man," they said, "an agitator among our nation, forbidding the payment of tribute to Caesar, and claiming himself to be an anointed king" (Luke 23:2 Weymouth).

The Christian Scriptures build on Jewish tradition about government. Instead of loyalty to the existing government there is a primary loyalty to God, who is the liberator from governmental and other forms of oppression. Christian loyalty is directed toward a servant king and the kingdom of God on earth. Jesus did not accept for himself the idea of either a warrior king or a king who ruled over subjects. The Gospels repeatedly refer to Jesus as Christ or Messiah, but Jesus himself apparently had reservations about the terms "Messiah" and "Son of God." "The Son of God" was originally the corporate body of Israel: "out of Egypt have I called my son" (Hosea 11:1). So also the term *Messiah* was a corporate one that could be applied to Israel. Jesus chose as his own title a unique phrase, "Son of man," which was not used by any revolutionary group or otherwise applied to the concept of Messiah. R. H. Strachan wrote that any prior "literary influence" on the use of "Son of man" comes from the vision of Daniel (Daniel 7:13f.).

In the book of Daniel the oppressed nation of Israel is symbolized by a human figure "like the Son of man," a frail human being in contrast with the four savage beasts armed with horns and claw, which represent the world powers to which it has been subjugated in past history. Israel appears in the likeness of a *man* "unarmed and inoffensive, incapable through any power of his own of making himself master of the world; he is only as a son of man. If ever he is to be master of the world, 'God must make him so.' "[9] The concept of a "son of man" is quite consistent with the Hebrew concept of a servant king who is drawn from the people to represent them against all the forces of oppression and who is also oppressed for their sake. Jesus contrasted the Gentile approval of government with this Jewish idea of a servant king or "son of man," in his statement:

> Those who are supposed to rule over the Gentiles lord it over them and their great men exercise authority over them. But it shall not be so among you: whoever wants to be great among you must be your servant. For the Son of man himself has not come to be served, but to serve and to give his life to set many others free (Mark 10:42-45).

Government apparently has one function, but Christians have another. Governors rule over other people, whereas the function of Christians is to liberate people from whatever it is that oppresses them.

Throughout the New Testament there is the functional or vocational difference between the punishment meted out by the secular government and the forgiveness expected from Christians. Paul in Romans 12 discusses the role of Christians, concluding with the admonition: "Beloved, never avenge yourselves, but leave it to the wrath of God." In the next chapter, in which he speaks of the governing authorities, he says that the magistrate is "the servant of God to execute his wrath on the wrongdoer." Quite clearly Christians were expected to operate differently from magistrates and men of wealth and political power. In other words, the early Christians envisioned a kind of parallel government, known as the kingdom of God. Its demands were much greater than those of the secular government it would eventually, in God's good time, replace.

New Testament writers nevertheless continued to look upon secular government as getting its authority from God, although it was not a perfect agent of God's will. Christians were not exempt from the minimum requirements of good conduct demanded by the law. They were to be "subject to the governing authorities," just as everyone else is. Paul's view of Roman government was that it was good and administered justice wisely. In Acts 23:12-30 and Acts 19:23-41 there are accounts of Paul and his associates being saved by Roman authorities from assault and murder. So it is not surprising that he believed Rome restrained lawlessness. On the other hand, Paul also said some negative things about government: "None of the ruler of this age understood" the purposes of God, "for if they had they would not have crucified the Lord of glory" (1 Corinthians 2:8). He asks Christians not to go into court with cases against each other, for the law is administered by "those who are least esteemed by the church" (1 Corinthians 6:4). Instead Christians are to judge their own cases or else suffer the wrong.

Paul obviously did not believe that every governmental authority was to be obeyed, because he and other apostles served time in prison. He also set up criteria by which to judge the state. In Romans 13 he said: "For rulers are not a terror to good works, but to evil." Suppose, however, that they are a terror to good works, as they were in crucifying Jesus? He also said that Christians should be subject "because of conscience," but what if conscience required disobedience?

Paul does not deal with such questions as "what if the magistrate is corrupt or tyrannical, or what if the man who does right is persecuted?" He was writing in the context of relatively good government. He was also apparently writing to Roman Christians about their specific situation. There is evidence that the Jews in Rome, Jewish Christians, were on the verge of armed revolt against the Romans at this time. The Roman historian Suetonius refers to disturbances in the capital during the reign of Claudius. Therefore, Paul's counsel in Romans 13 to pay taxes and not to resist the authorities must be seen as an effort to conteract the Zealot tendencies and is more an argument against armed revolt than a general statement that all governments are always to be obeyed.

The political authorities are not to be resisted because they exist and function under the authority of God, Paul said (Romans 13:1f.). Many Christians over the centuries have understood this not as a call to absolute obedience to the state but as encouragement to resist tyrants who have ordained themselves and function in rejection of the authority of God. Paul is also concerned that the Christian teaching of freedom from the Jewish law and from religious legalism not be used as an argument against obeying secular government. So he writes that love fulfills the law (Romans 13:10) and counsels against specific acts such as "rioting and drunkenness (Romans 13:13).

Paul was not asserting, however, that God empowered government to set a Christian's moral standards or give political guidance to the church. Rather, since all authority comes from God, the state is something that God can use or overrule for his own purposes. As John Howard Yoder points out:

> The Christian is called not to *obey* the state, which would imply actually receiving from the state his moral guidance, but to be *subject*, which means simply that he shall not rebel or seek to act if the state were not there. Whether he obeys the state or

finds that his submission must be in the form of disobedience and accepting punishment for it will depend on what the state asks of him.[10]

Although the early Christians thought of themselves as subject to the rulers of their age so long as the age lasted, they did not believe in unconditional obedience. Peter and the apostles, for example, refused to obey the authorities, asserting "we must obey God rather than men" (Acts 5:29). The commands of the political authorities never excused a departure from their commitment to the kingdom of God, whether the government tried to prevent preaching or demanded military service or a loyalty oath to Caesar. Jesus apparently sanctioned civil disobedience in forbidding his followers to deny him before kings and governors. As C. J. Cadoux pointed out, refusal to disobey his ethical teaching at Caesar's bidding would be but a natural extension of this precept.[11] Jesus himself was crucified because of his refusal to accept either the deified state projected by Jewish nationalists or the deified state of the Romans. And it was Caesar who martyred Paul, Peter, and thousands of other early Christians.

The persecution of Chrisians is the subject of the book of Revelation. It provides a different perspective from Paul's view of Roman government as relatively good. Revelation was probably written in the days of the Emperor Domitian after the Roman government had changed. Domitian persecuted Christians and, according to Tertullian and the tradition of a hundred years later, had John brought to Rome where he was examined and tortured, then sent to the convict island of Patmos.[12] John described the Emperor as a beast who blasphemes God and causes all who will not worship him to be slain (Revelation 13:15). John also specifically approved of civil disobedience by all those who refused to yield to the Roman government (Revelation 20:4).

The teachings of Jesus, Paul, and John are directly related to Jesus' confrontation with the political powers of his day and their religious collaborators, because these were the powers responsible for the subjugation of the people.

The political message of the New Testament with respect to government can be summarized as follows: Jesus sees himself as living out the role of a liberator in the tradition of a servant-king who speaks for and suffers in the place of those who are oppressed. This necessarily involves him in conflict with established government because he advocates complete loyalty to the kingdom of God, which is to supplant existing Jewish and Roman governments.

The conflict between Jesus and Caesar, which is seen more clearly in the Crucifixion and in the events leading to it, is either present from the very beginning of his life or else Matthew and Luke were so impressed by the conflict that they interpreted the events of his birth in terms of Jesus' conflict with Caesar. The followers of Jesus after the Crucifixion also taught and lived a life of conflict with government. This did not mean braking the law unless the law required disobedience to their commitment to the kingdom of God. In other respects they were to be more virtuous than the law required.

Paul made use of the Roman government to protect himself in his travels and permit him to preach the gospel. However, Paul did spend time in prison and did teach Christians not to participate in the existing government.

A life devoted to liberation or to the kingdom of God necessarily means disobedience to oppressive systems, including governments that dominate rather than serve the people. Civil disobedience in the New Testament was always open and nonviolent. Violence was an aspect of dominance and not a characteristic of service. But the early Christians also saw their conflict with powers or systems rather than with persons as such. So Paul said. " . . . our fight is not against any physical enemy; it is against organizations and powers . . . " (Ephesians 6:12 Phillips). Another translation of the same statement says, "For ours is not a conflict with mere flesh and blood but with the despotisms, the empires, the forces that control and govern . . . " (Weymouth).

The New Testament does not provide a systematic analysis of politics or government. It assumed the existence of government and the need for liberation from it. Although it developed strategies of accommodation to government and strategies of disobedience, it did not propose a political program for the overthrow of the Roman Empire or for achieving the kingdom of God they desired. That was not something the

early Christians felt they could determine, other than by obedience to the kingdom rather than existing structures.

4

POLITICAL REALISM

Modern states, like ancient political communities, are not voluntary. People are born into them and few consciously choose to migrate to another political community. Even those who emigrate find themselves in the presence of a government whose activity or coercion the individual cannot escape. The dream of a society with little or no governmental oppression is still a dream.

Governments exist in theory to maintain order and provide justice. These are accomplished by law. The law, in effect, is the will of the government and is evident in the decisions that it makes and enforces. In principle, law ought to define and delimit the power and scope of government quite as much as it defines the duties or forbidden activities of the people. But in practice law reflects and defends the interests of a ruling class. In a capitalist society property values tend to be more important than persons. In a Communist society persons are subordinated to the interests of the party or the preservation of the power of those in the upper levels of the party. In both societies the security and advancement of the state is more important than the lives of all the citizens, as is evident in preparations for nuclear war that could destroy two-thirds or more of the total population of each nation.

Law in every society ought to serve persons and make politically real the dignity or worth that inheres in each person. The United States Constitution assumes a valid privacy for each and every person that may not be invaded by the state unless a court issues a warrant based on "probable cause" and "particularly describing the place to be searched and the persons or things to be seized."

In practice, the nation's law enforcement agencies, including the F.B.I. and various police departments, infiltrate organizations, harass persons belonging or contributing to those groups, disrupt their organizations, and in some cases steal their property.[1]

Unequal justice is the rule with every administration in Washington, in spite of the fact that the Constitution provides for a theoretical equality of every citizen before the law. In practice, high government officials and corporate business leaders are given special treatment so that they are not required to pay much if any penalty for serious crimes. For example, former President Richard Nixon, his vice president, Spiro Agnew, and former attorney general Richard Kleindienst were given special treatment so they were not required to pay any penalty. A conscientious objector who refuses to injure anyone, however, is sent to prison for several years for an infraction of the Selective Service Law.

President Ford, who had announced prior to his pardon of Richard Nixon that he would not pardon or grant an amnesty to those who had refused to participate in an undeclared war against Vietnam, justified such unequal treatment by saying he had consulted God and his own conscience.

Unequal justice in the United States is not limited to special treatment for those members of the ruling class who are caught in their violation of the law. The entire governmental system operates for the benefit of the rich and powerful. A number of wealthy individuals and corporations pay no income taxes, chiefly because of loopholes the Congress and the President provide in the tax laws. Others pay relatively low taxes. Serious tax discrimination occurs at many other points. For example, unearned investment income subject to capital gains tax or corporation income is taxed at only a fraction of the tax rate applied to the hard earned income of those who work for a living. Tax deductions are also more generous for industrialists for repairing and replacing machinery than for workers who need to repair themselves through medical, dental, or hospital treatment.

The people pay taxes to subsidize the enormous profits of the five hundred large corporations that appear regularly on the Pentagon's list of prime military contractors. They also pay taxes to provide federal subsidies to large landowners, concessions to oil companies, and subsidies to various other business and private persons while the poor are being deprived of food stamps. Nancy Amidei, director of the Washington-based Food Research and Action Center, said in 1981, "The average food stamp benefit is $1.30 per person per day. That doesn't even pay for peanut butter these days. You have a hard time feeding kids . . . on $1.30 a day."[2]

It is not surprising that some political scientists view all government as operating in the interest of the upper economic classes. Harold Laski, a British political scientist, has written:

> It may be taken as a general rule that the character of any particular state will be, broadly speaking, a function of the economic system which obtains in the society it controls. Any social system reveals itself as a struggle for the control of economic power, since those who possess the power are able, in the measure of their possession, to make their wants effective. Law then becomes a system of relations giving the expression of legal form to their wants. . . . The legal order is a mask behind which a dominant economic interest secures the benefit of political authority. The state as it operates does not deliberately seek general justice or general utility (welfare) but the interest, in the largest sense, of the dominant class in society.[3]

Those who claim that the state necessarily operates in the interest of a dominant economic or other class instead of in the interest of the whole people are called "realists." They believe that self-interest, the struggle for power, organization into power groups to control society, and special privileges to those who gain control cannot be structured out of existence. Insofar as these persons think theologically they would give priority to the nature of persons as sinners and competitors and pay little attention to the possibility of repentance or to the power involved in commitment to liberation.

The realist holds that both persons and states are basically motivated by self-interest and are fundamentally aggressive. Aggressiveness must be deterred by either some check or balance, or counter aggression.

There are, however, certain fallacies in this position. One is that not all individuals are aggressive. Millions of persons are rather docile even in the face of grave injustice and do not revolt against exploiting systems or governments. If we accept the idea that persons are at birth self-centered, it does not mean that such self-interest is always or even usually evident in political conflict, such as action against elites who deprive them of freedom or dignity.

A second fallacy is to root aggression or the struggle for power in the individual instead of in political and economic systems or environmental or other problems. Aggressiveness or struggle by large groups of people is almost always the result of frustration and the long experience of abuses. An experience of injustice or a deep sense of frustration may reach a point that is no longer regarded as acceptable. At that point a challenge to the *status quo* may be made by an otherwise unaggressive or cautious person or group.

This suggests a third weakness in the realist theory that aggression and the struggle for power are rooted in the individual. Rousseau believed that the lone individual who was able in a primitive condition to meet his own needs was not aggressive or intent upon conflict. The realist, on the other hand, jumps to the conclusion that because some persons in social groups engage in conflict to achieve wealth or power, aggression is an aspect of human nature. In practice most human beings who are citizens of states tend to be nonaggressive toward their governments and each other except when greatly provoked. It is difficult to generalize about all persons on the basis of those who are aggressive or nonaggressive in society. Moreover, the Christian concept of all persons as sinners, borrowed by the realist, does not imply that sin is always or usually demonstrated in a particular form such as overt conflict. It may be manifest in restrained envy or obsequious, self-serving activity. The realist, of course, stops short of accepting the Christian analysis that it is possible to be liberated from self-centeredness or any particular manifestation of it and to join with others in serving universal rather than parochial interests.

The opposite pole to that of realism is idealism. This approach to politics is based on the assumption that self-interest, the struggle for power, and power elites can be brought under some kind of discipline or control, generally as a result of overall structural reform.

The term "idealist" would include a number of apparently unrelated positions. It would include the Christian who believes that the way to change society is to convert individuals, especially influential ones, to Christianity. This position implies that persons with high ethical standards will make any system an approximation of the good society.

The fallacy in this position is that Christian bankers, industrialists, labor leaders, and politicians do not seek to change the system but to work within it. If a banker were to take seriously his obligation as a Christian to help those in need by providing loans to the poor at little or no interest, while charging higher rates to the rich, he would soon cease to be a banker. Economic, political, and social systems have dynamics of their own, so that it was necessary to abolish economic systems known as slavery and feudalism, instead of simply trying to make slave owners or feudal lords into moral men.

The term "idealist" would include the Marxist who believes that it is the capitalist organization of society that is the root of the struggle for power. For example, competition arises from a struggle over markets and raw materials. Such a Marxist also believes that a socialist or Communist restructuring of society will not only eliminate the evils of capitalism but by definition avoid competition, struggles for power, and even war. There is, however, ample evidence that such struggles for power have not been eliminated either within or between existing Marxist states.

There are, of course, socialists who make no idealist claims but simply view some form of democratic socialism as a better society with fewer major evils than exist under capitalism.

The term "idealism" would also include those who believe that the American way of life and the economic advantages of our middle class existence are so integrally related to democracy and universally desirable that they ought to be exported everywhere, replacing other cultures, economies, and political systems. They tend to gloss over the disadvantages of American capitalism or to ignore the racism, militarism, and political inequality that exist in American society by idealizing the concept of democracy, which is very imperfectly realized even within its stronghold, the middle class.

The fact that the late Reinhold Niebuhr labeled himself a Christian realist does not mean that he or other realists are actually more realistic or perceptive about politics than idealists. Nor does it mean that he was not also infectecd with idealism.

Consider, for example, his statement, "Democracy as a political institution is rooted in the principle of universal suffrage, which arms every citizen with political power and the chance to veto the actions of his rulers."[4] This of course, is an oversimplification. Women had the power of the vote since 1919 and black males in the North more than five decades before that, yet neither group has had the power of veto or achieved freedom or equality, which are the essence of democracy. Niebuhr identified the legal or formal right to vote with real political power. He did not acknowledge in such a statement the excessive power of wealth or corporate interests, but implied that once every two or four years by voting there is a real check on the power of the giant corporations and the wealthy few in our society.

The realist is heir to Machiavelli's thought, which was primarily responsible for the divorce of political behavior from the theological assumption that there is one God guiding the world and therefore an intelligible purpose and goal. This theological assumption means that politics as well as all other activity must be guided by the rationality and goodness of that purpose. Machiavelli is responsible for the idea that politics is autonomous, having no relationship to individual morality or cosmic purpose. He implied that there might be no ultimate purpose or goal in the world and that politics had an end that was valid in itself, which justified everything else done in its name. The goal of politics to Machiavelli was the welfare of the particular state to which he gave his allegiance. His morality was tied up with the success of his political unit.

Modern political realists are primarily concerned, as was Machiavelli, with the national interest of their own nation-state. In practice this means support for a predominance of national economic and military power. The term "national interest" is really a euphemism for the economic interests of the dominant business groups and the strategic interests of the armed forces, which in contemporary America and many other industrialized countries are so allied as to be included in the designation "military-industrial complex." Realists are not prepared to withdraw their support from American political, economic, and military interests that oppress people at home and abroad. Those interests often prefer to work with political dictators or feudal economic oligarchies in other countries.

Secretary of State Kissinger espoused the realist position in a Senate hearing on July 24, 1974, when he opposed moves in Congress to bar military and economic aid to the South Korean dictator Park Chung Hee, who was arresting and sentencing to death clergymen, university professors, and other critics of his repression. Kissinger pointed to South Korea's strategic position and said, "Where we believe the national interest is at stake, we proceed even when we don't approve" of a country's policies.[5]

President Jimmy Carter, despite his publicized emphasis on human rights, followed the same approach not only in South Korea but in the Philippines, Iran, South Africa, and other repressive states. Such a position equates the national interest with support of a particular dictatorship and runs the risk of anti-U.S. policies if the people revolt, as they did in Thailand in October, 1973, or if events drive dictators out of power, as in Greece in July 1974, or Iran in 1979.

Realists in practice accept, and some even approve, such oppression because they recognize that realism demands both a stable atmosphere in which American business can freely operate and "reliable" allies with whom U.S. armed forces can cooperate. The political and Christian realists support the use of armed power to maintain the national interest and hence the status quo, instead of asking that national power be used to support revolutionary activity in behalf of the oppressed people of other nations. Power, to the realist, is not the ability to induce change for the benefit of the oppressed everywhere but the ability to impose a nation's will on others.

The Christian realist accommodates Christianity to this realist position and the whole Machiavellian emphasis on the autonomy of politics by seeking forgiveness for such a political position rather than empowerment to avoid such support of power politics and oppression, and also by encouraging resignation to these conditions. Reinhold Niebuhr wrote:

> It is possible for individuals to be saved from this sinful pretension, not by achieving an absolute perspective upon life but by their recognition of their inability to do so. Individuals may be saved by repentance, which is the gateway to grace. The recognition of creatureliness and finiteness, in other words, may

become the basis of man's reconciliation to God through his resignation to his finite condition.[6]

Christian realists, in other words, find it unrealistic to do anything but give support to imperialism, war, and oppressive systems, resigning themselves to a finite and sinful condition.

Christian realism differs from political realism only insofar as Christian values are held in the offing as ultimate norms. Christians also rely on God's continuing forgiveness for their continuing sin.

This acceptance of repeated cycles of oppressive economic, political, or military action, followed by divine forgiveness, "reminds one of the barbarians of the great migrations, who murdered and did penance for it, till penance became an actual technique for enabling murder to be done. Ivan the Terrible behaved in exactly this way."[7]

It is possible for those committed to a politics of liberation to accept a part of the realist premise without accepting the whole position. The valid aspect of realism is this: that politics is the arena in which power groups and powerful individuals struggle to achieve their own desires. This human struggle cannot be structured out of existence. However, those engaged in a politics of liberation do not accept the ideological premises of power politics or the priority of the national interest as over against either the interest of a world community or the welfare of oppressed people in other countries. Neither do they support or acquiesce in the control of government by a financial, industrial, or military elite. Resistance to such control is a genuinely realistic way of making it seem imperative to government leaders to engage in social change.

Those engaged in the politics of liberation are not idealists in the sense that they envision perfect or near-perfect structures that will eliminate all oppression. They do, however, believe in structural change. They assume that oppression in a complex society is institutionalized in systems, that the elimination or transformation of specific systems can end or minimize specific forms of oppression, and that there is a need for a continuing effort that is sometimes called "permanent revolution."

Traditional Protestant and Roman Catholic thought introduce another dimension of the nature of government. The idea that government is primarily intended to preserve order and originated because of human sinfulness is a traditional Protestant theory. This is the idea that the sin of humans would lead to self-destruction and chaos if the state were not present to restrain them. Over against this is the traditional Roman Catholic idea, derived from Aristotelian thought, that government arises from the social and communitarian nature of persons who are called to cooperate with each other to achieve justice or the common good. There is some merit in both positions. Even the maintenance of order is impossible without some degree of justice.

The state as it is organized today, however, does not exist for the purpose of equal justice for all its citizens. Neither does it exist to liberate the oppressed. In spite of all theory to the contrary about the state, it is organized to maintain law and order for the benefit of the ruling class. As Jesus suggested, the rulers of government engage in domination, not servanthood. In other words, God's political purpose is not encompassed in the state or in keeping order but in the process of liberation. This occurs in and through the community of the oppressed. It is not government, as such, that is the agent of justice or equality. Those who are excluded from the ruling elite and who are conscious of their oppression must continually demand the liberation and respect that is due them as human beings. It is the oppressed, who are set over against the ruling class by the nature of their condition, that keep governments aware of the need for justice. It is the accommodation of governments to the spoken or unspoken demands of the oppressed that leads to any promotion of the general welfare.

Still another aspect of the nature of government is its legal monopoly of the instruments of violence. In any political jurisdiction there cannot be two or more legal centers of armed power without the danger of civil war. Governments normally do not tolerate private armies. Some governments do not permit citizens to possess guns. The United States, however, is so capitalistic in its orientation that it permits the sale of various weapons for profit to anyone who can afford to buy them. It has such a violent and lawless tradition that no serious effort is made to prevent armed violence against either animals or humans. The American Rifle Association is the lobby for gun interests. The Pentagon also encourages the possession of weapons by those who will train in markmanship. The Symbionese Liberation Army in 1973 openly bought army surplus M-1 rifles that they converted to automatic weapons, Mauser automatic pistols designed for combat, sawed-off shotguns, and other weapons. These weapons were used on a public rifle range near San Francisco before they were used against human targets. The F.B.I. estimates that 95 million Americans own guns. This implies that most households in the U.S. are armed.

In the United States the government monopoly of armed force is purely formal, being used only to prevent the formation of large organized armies as distinct from smaller armed gangs. For example, New York State legislative investigators reported the existence of 315 gangs in New York City, with 8,061 verified members and an overall total of 19,503 members. The report states that there was an average of 37 gang incidents and 62 arrests every week during the year. Weapons included large quantities of automatic rifles, pistols, grenades, army bazookas, and mortars. Gang members engage in guerrilla-type raids, intimidate school administrators to change the curriculum "in favor of the gangs' needs and desires," and intimidate "city officials to obtain employment, recreational facilities, and benefits." They also "engage in shakedowns of area merchants and residents. . . ."[8]

Nevertheless, one of the marks of sovereignty is that the state is theoretically or legally entitled to a monoply of armed force. The state presumably needs such a monopoly to maintain order. In the United States, however, order does not mean the same thing that it does in some countries in which the safety of every person is important. Order in the United States means the maintenance of security for major systems and structures, including the property of the country's businesses. There is little protection of persons or property in the black ghetto or poor white districts and no serious effort to prevent violence against other Americans. The major effort is directed at the apprehension and imprisonment of those who have actually violated the law and not the prevention of violence in the first place.

It seems evident from an analysis of government in the United States that it is both an instrument of oppression and an agent of law and order. It is more likely to maintain order for the affluent and powerful, but it is also likely to do so for the oppressed when they are organized to demand it and are able to communicate their plight of unequal justice adequately to the general population. It requires a highly politicized minority, in combination with other similar minorities, to produce any reaction from the nonpoliticized middle class, so aptly described by Richard Nixon as "the silent majority." By this he probably meant that they would tolerate almost anything the government did so long as it did not directly attack their own privileges.

Even when government keeps order chiefly for business and the middle and upper classes, it is better, according to some, than the absence of order that would occur if there were a complete breakdown of all law, and rule by mob action. Political writers and theologians all too often make such justification of government. It is nevertheless inadequate for a politics or liberation. Governments that primarily reflect the will of a privileged minority or majority are oppressive and carry within themselves the seeds for eventual disorder for everyone. Even at the risk of some disorder it is the function of liberation movements to avoid collaboration with oppressive governments, to encourage the organization of minorities to change political and economic systems and their elites, and, when necessary, to stimulate people to withdraw consent from government or otherwise resist it. The right to resist oppression is the key to legitimate government. The state has no *a priori* claim to allegiance. Its claim depends on the degree to which it minimizes oppression and meets the needs of its citizens, including its minorities. Nonviolent liberation movements contribute to law and order more than does any oppressive government. This is because law and order are sustained best by the cooperation of people with their government. Such cooperation is in turn a byproduct of freedom, justice, and equality so that people are not alienated from their government.

Although government tends to operate in the interest of powerful economic units, it is essential to recognize that there are opposing economic interests and theories. Political forces can bring and have brought economic interests under control, especially when those economic interests are themselves divided, but also when the social power of masses of people is focused in united action on the government. The question of what constitutes effective power is therefore always crucial for those who are oppressed, as well as for the administrators of government.

POLITICAL POWER

The English word "power" comes from the French word *pouvoir*, and the Latin *posse*, both of which mean "to be able." There is a sense in which "being" and "power" are identical. To be able to live or to persist in being is to have power, whereas only death or nonexistence is identical with powerlessness.

Power differs from strength. When we speak of the strength of steel we refer to a quality by which it can endure stress or the application of force without breaking. Human beings have both physical and moral strength in their ability to endure stress or withstand pressure. But strength in anything that lives also refers to a quality inherent in a person or thing that enables it to exert force. Force is not identical with violence but can be defined generally as the use of energy. Violence is the act or process of violating the rights or personhood of others through physical or psychological abuse. It is possible also to do violence to animals, the environment, and property.

There is such a thing as armed force, but there is also unarmed physical force, as well as moral force, or what Gandhi called *Satyagraha* or truth force.

When we talk about political power, we find there is no universally acceptable definition. Many sociologists and political scientists would define such power as the capacity to impose control over others by the threat or use of some kind of penalty. Karl Mannheim wrote that power "is every action that compels certain action in others."[1] The world "compel" is crucial. It means "to force compliance or to cause irresistibly." Power, when identified with compulsion or control over people, implies the capacity to make them do something against their will.

Another definition of political power is simply the ability of any political leader or unit to accomplish a purpose. This definition is a more general, and therefore more inclusive, one.

It does not, for example, rule out forms of power that persuade or influence rather than compel. It recognizes that it is possible to influence human behavior or cause people to act in a desired way without threat of punishment or actual penalty.

Political power can also be defined as the will of individual persons or groups exercising decisive influence on the collective life of a number of people.

Governments have many ways of exercising power. They can compel the obedience of people by the threat or actual use of armed force. They can also persuade people by the written or spoken word. "Knowledge is power," wrote Francis Bacon, and Samuel Johnson indicated that "knowledge is more than equivalent to force." Another Englishman, Edward Bulwer-Lytton, is responsible for the phrase "The pen is mightier than the sword." So political or economic control over the press or television is a form of power.

Governments can also exercise power by inducement. If a government wants to increase rice production, it can offer a guaranteed price higher than the usual or current price of rice. One government can even induce another government to build a certain road or engage in a certain program by offering to pay a part of the cost. We can define inducement as the offer of certain advantages to another, conditional on compliance with what you propose. Governments can prevent or stop a revolt of the people by improving their standard of living or otherwise meeting their demands for human dignity, equality of treatment, employment, housing, or food.

Governmental and, in fact, all political power is based on the ability to influence the behavior of people or, in other words, to accomplish a purpose. We must, therefore, not make the mistake of identifying power with any one form of power. There is, nevertheless, a tendency on the part of many people to identify power with physical might or armed force.

In general, power may be classified as either coercive or persuasive. The word "coercion" comes from the Latin *coercere* which means "to shut up, enclose, or encircle." To coerce is to compel by force, threat, or other pressure. Persuasion involves changing the mind or will so that a person acts from a new conviction. Coercion, on the other hand, means making people act as you want without changing their convictions, or while they continue to hold convictions contrary to yours.

Although coercive and persuasive forms of power seem to be mutually exclusive, it is possible to combine them. Both Gandhi and Martin Luther King used a type of nonviolent direct action that was coercive in its approach but designed to change the will of their opponents so they operated from a new or higher insight. Because their coercion was nonviolent, their opponents were assured from the onset that there was no ultimate threat to their physical existence. They were, therefore, able to face the issues involved in the conflict rather than be primarily concerned about their own safety or security. The fact that Gandhi and King were genuinely and positively concerned for the well-being of their opponents, even to the point of never taking unfair advantage of them, was a persuasive factor. The Gandhian approach is not an attempt to control opponents or gain a victory over them. Rather, it is an attempt to restructure the political situation or the system so as to better meet the human needs of both groups. Although Gandhi's method is unique in that it combines coercion and persuasion in one method or form of power, we must be aware that governments that have no Gandhian motivation sometimes use coercion and persuasion at the same time.

We can make certain assertions about political power. The first is that it is *generalized.* By this we mean that one display of power is not enough. It must be capable of being exercised again and again or must have what we call "staying" or lasting power. One illustration of the ability to accomplish purpose is not enough, especially if it is followed by one failure after another. There is a sense in which political power grows out of success. It must also be generalized in that people comply with the wishes of those exercising power not solely by virtue of one approach to power, such as military coercion. If political power is based solely on superior armed force, it is unlikely to last. There must be some element of identification of the will of the people with the will of their political leaders. Physical force in itself could not hold a complex society together. That identification of interest is won by appeals to patriotism or national or class interest, or by some other method of persuasion that arouses loyalty.

A second assertion follows from the first, that political

power is generalized only if it is structured or institutionalized. Julius Caesar had military power, not simply because of his charismatic leadership or his brilliant mind but because of the organization and discipline of the Roman army. Stalin had power and Mao had power because of the disciplined organization of the Communist Party. If any person or group is to have a purpose or direction or be able again and again to accomplish a purpose, there must be a mechanism or organization through which its resources are mobilized to achieve effective collective action.

In any political structure the legal right to command obedience is known as *authority*. Power differs from authority in that authority is delegated or recognized by others. Gilbert Chesterton is responsible for a story that distinguishes power from authority. Some men were sitting in a restaurant when an elephant walked in. One of the men said he acknowledged the power of the elephant to throw him out of the restaurant but not his authority. The elected president of a nation, legislators who represent the people, police who are appointed to enforce the laws can all be said to have an authority by virtue of their delegated position. There is, of course, an authority that does not come from either an election or a delegated position but from tradition, as in the case of a king who inherits the throne, or from conquest in war or revolution. Mao gained his authority by virtue of being the military leader and spokesman for the Communist Party. Napoleon had similar authority as conqueror and emperor of France.

Some people in history have attained political authority because of the love or admiration of the people. Gandhi is one of those who did. Gandhi's authority was not derived from being head of an organization but from being a leader whose spiritual and political capacities were generally admired and recognized by the people. When India achieved independence, Gandhi had more authority than did the newly elected prime minister, Nehru.

Governments themselves usually have both authority and power. It is *legitimacy* that gives authority to what the government does. Legitimacy is the general consent given to a government by the people. *Consent* does not mean that the people approve of every act of a government. It does mean that the government itself is generally acceptable. Governments that have lost the consent of the people have to rule more by armed force than authority.

Real power in politics stems from the love of the people for their government. Or perhaps it is more accurate to speak of their confidence in and loyalty to their government. Under these circumstances governments do not need to use armed force against their people. The possibility of force or coercion belongs to power, but the less force is used, the more power there is. In the heavily industrialized cities of northern Italy and in the black ghettoes of the United States the police travel in teams of two to four. They are heavily armed with club, revolver, carbine, or shotgun, and often with tear gas or Mace. Where the government has no *real* power, it has to display such armed power as it has. In London, however, where the people look upon the government as their servant, the police are affectionately known as "bobbies." One bobby unarmed can go anywhere in London, day or night. In England the government has the consent of the people.

It can be argued that everyone in London knows that the unarmed bobbies could be immediately armed, and that they are also backed up by an effective armed force of British soldiers. This does not, of course, mean that the ultimate power of government resides in its armed forces. Rather, it means that a relatively small police force or army may be needed to deal with an exceptional instance of violence. At one time in New York City there were 18,000 police and 8 million New Yorkers. The 18,000, however well-armed, could not control the entire eight million or even one-tenth of them. The police force was able to function because most of the people accepted the police as their agents, or as necessary to the direction of traffic and the control of crime. The police are not powerful because of their guns but because they have an authority derived from the people. Generally speaking, the police never number more than one fourth of one per cent of the people in any city or state in the nation. There are about 2.4 police per 1,000 population in cities of more than 250,000 people. More than half the police in the United States are concentrated in fewer than 50 cities with a population exceeding 250,000. So the police cannot by sheer force maintain laws that the people are unwilling to obey.

When they cease to be agents of the people and are used against the people, they lose their authority and become mere purveyors of armed force, as has happened so frequently in black communities across the United States.

Coercive force by government is based on the assumption that a relatively small minority, rather than a majority, of the people will engage in violence or other breaking of the law. If a majority or significant minority were to break one or more laws consistently, those laws would have to be changed or the government would be in crisis. Government, in the final analysis, rests on the consent and cooperation of the people.

We can go so far as to say that the people in any nation so obviously abhor physical coercion by governments that in almost every episode where it is used the government either tries to keep most of the people from knowing about it or attempts to justify it morally. The United States tried to justify armed action against the Dominican Republic and Vietnam by indicating that it was in the interests of freedom. The Soviet Union justified its armed action in Afghanistan by claims that it was invited to intervene and by assertions about outside imperialist powers wanting to control the country.

Any commentary on power should take note of the limitations of human power. No human being, system, or government is all-powerful. Every physically powerful athlete feels a kind of panic at the thought of becoming ill with influenza or some other disease or weakness on the day of an important match or contest. The Rockefeller family in the United States is financially very powerful, but all the Rockefellers in the world could not jointly have appointed the successor to either Mao Zedong or Pope Paul VI. The pope is very powerful in the Roman Catholic Church, but he cannot prevent Roman Catholics from violating his pronouncements on birth control, abortion, and certain other issues. The United States is probably the greatest military power in human history, but it was unable to use that power effectively against North Vietnam, though it did so against both Germany and Japan during World War II. North Vietnam had less than a tenth of the population of the United States. It had no navy, no air force, no chemical industry. As the world judges power, it was weak.

Even totalitarian governments are limited in their power.

The Polish government cannot crush the Roman Catholic Church in that country. In China during the Cultural Revolution the political forces of Mao combined with the military forces of Marshal Lin Piao could not finally destroy Mao's opponents in the Party or remake the Party and its bureaucracy. The present government is heir to the compromises that had to be made between Mao, the military, the Party, and the various governmental bureaucracies.

In the Soviet Union and Yugoslavia the various governments have had to come to terms with their unorganized peasants. The attempt to force complete collectivization of the land has failed because of the resistance of the peasants. Lenin, Stalin, Tito, and others had to bow to peasant demands for private plots of ground.

Chester Bowles wrote, "Since 1947, 1.2 billion people—half of mankind— have generated enough effective power to change their form of government, although the substance of what we have so largely come to accept as power was in each case on the side of the status quo."[2] Bowles was referring chiefly to colonial peoples or those under dictatorships allied with major powers. We must keep in mind that the overwhelming number of former colonies gained their freedom against superior military might chiefly by the use of nonviolent means.

Both persons and systems that seem tremendously powerful are sometimes confounded by what seems to be very weak. A snowflake is so weak it will melt on a person's wrist, but the engulfing snowdrifts of a Russian winter routed Napoleon's armies. In both nature and politics it can be said, in biblical terms, that "God has chosen the weak things of the world to confound the things which are mighty," and "it was what the world calls low and insignificant and unreal that God chose to nullify its realities . . . (1 Corinthians 1:27f.). These words of the apostle Paul graphically describe the limitations of everything that claims to be powerful.

As has already been suggested, governmental violence against citizens has its limitations. Yet violence for many people is the "ultimate power," the decisive factor in political change. Mao Zedong has summarized it in the phrase "Power grows out of the barrel of a gun." Such a phrase was natural in the mouth of a military man who had become accustomed over the years to fighting rival troops. In that respect the possession of guns is power because they can destroy enemies who, if they were to live, would destroy your troops. But guns in themselves are not power. Guns, of course, are only instruments in the hands of people. If the people with guns refuse to shoot, the guns have no power. Power resides in people. This means that those planning violent revolution must be able to win and maintain the cooperation of the people they want to use the guns. In other words, violence is not the essence of power but the instrument of power. Even those who possess guns have no power unless those at whom the guns are pointed are willing to obey. In the case of a person threatened by a gun, that person must consent before there is any exercise of power. If the person at whom the gun is pointed will not do the will of the one who is armed, the latter has no ability to accomplish his purpose and hence no power. It can be argued that there is the power to kill. But what happens if a revolutionary band threatens a hundred or a thousand peasants or workers if they don't produce food or weapons for them? Can the violent band kill them and still make revolution credible to other workers or peasants? It makes no difference whether the guns are held by revolutionaries or defenders of the status quo. Some form of consent is essential to all exercises of power. The ultimate form of political power is not violence but the numbers of people who are committed tenaciously to a common purpose.

Karl Marx, from whose doctrine both Lenin and Mao departed at crucial points, was more perceptive in his understanding of power as distinct from violence. Marx repudiated the bourgeois notion, imbedded in the political rationale for the English, American, and French revolutions, that the violent seizure of governmental machinery can transform society. Instead, he held that the social and political process would create the conditions that he called a revolutionary situation. The situation developed or unfolded as a result of the internal contradictions of the system. In some societies such as England and the United States no violence would be necessary. In others, if it was necessary, it would be no more needed or significant than the kind of assistance a midwife gives to the birth of a baby that had already developed to the point of starting to leave the womb. Erich Fromm in his book *Marx's Concept of Man* wrote of Marx:

> It is exactly one of his great insights that Marx transcends the traditional middle-class concept—he did *not* believe in the creative power of force, in the idea that political force of itself could create a new social order. For this reason, (armed) force, for Marx, could have at most only a transitory significance, never the role of a permanent element in the transformation of society.[4]

Mao and Lenin have at this point of political violence departed from Marx to accept the traditional middle-class idea of violence as power to deal with evil. It is this middle-class ideology about violence that so many minority and Third World peoples have learned from the Western democracies, who also furnish them weapons at a profit. They have accepted the idea that violence is power without questioning its assumptions or analyzing carefully its consequences. Black intellectuals who have accepted middle-class values at other points have been especially vulnerable to the acceptance of the way of violence as well. It is significant that Martin Luther King, who started with these assumptions and at first had armed guards around his house in Montgomery, repudiated violence as power after careful study and the challenge of his Christian commitment to love. Instead he became the leader of the most significant non-violent movement in the Western world.

Power is found in love or caring for people so that they want to cooperate with those who are concerned for their well-being. It is found in the cooperation of people, especially masses of people. Leaders who point guns at people and order them around are in the process of alienating the people on whom their power depends.

Many of the assumptions about the relationship of power and violence come from primitive analyses of nature, which is assumed to be highly competitive and violent. T. H. Huxley in 1888 gave credence to the idea that the strongest, swiftest, and most cunning of animals survive. Peter Kropotkin responded with a series of articles, later published in his book *Mutual Aid: A Factor in Evolution*, in which he demonstrated that competition among animals is limited, that animals thrive by the avoidance or elimination of competition and by substituting mutual aid and support. Birds migrate south in winter to avoid competition when food is scarce. Some animals hibernate and others store food for the winter to avoid competition. He asserted that natural selection favors the various species that know how to avoid competition, such as ants that combine in nests, and rodents that gather in villages.

Professor Herman J. Muller in his presidential address at the Eighth International Congress of Genetics, held in July 1948 in Stockholm, stated:

> Man's intelligence, however, has won its victories chiefly because it was a cooperative one, and it would not have been such had there been no strong fellow-feeling. It is the attachment of mother for child, of man for woman, and of man for man, that has bound us into the little groups that won, and . . . it is this basic feeling of love that will continue to make the living world go round, if go it does. It is this for which we must readily put forth sacrifice.[5]

Ashley Montagu, the anthropologist, points out:

> All organisms come into being from other organisms. Whether they are reproduced asexually or sexually, all organisms in the process of coming into being are for a time dependent upon and interdependent with the organism from which they are being generated. Whatever happens to the one happens to the other. The needs of the one are satisfied by the other. . . . It is in this process of dependence and interdependency, the reproductive process, that the meaning of the origin and nature of social life, of cooperation, is to be sought.[6]

There seems to be ample evidence to sustain the thesis that conflict, competition, and all forms of struggle are possible in our world only because of a deeper or more basic cooperation that sustains life. If it were not for this substructure of love and cooperation, or what theologically might be called "the ground of being," the various forms of conflict and competition would lead to anarchy and unlimited destruction. Even violence, insofar as it relies on weapons, depends upon cooperation in both their production and use.

The term "love" is not to be understood in its sentimental or romantic sense. It is not fondness for a specific person, but concern for the well-being of another or respect for the human worth of one so like one's self. Cooperation involves mutual support or the working together for a mutual purpose. The affirmation that love and cooperation are essential to all life and basic to political communities is a repudiation of the idea that political power is to be identified with the ability to dominate or destroy. It means that the purpose of power is not to make other persons powerless but to empower or share power so as to increase the possibility of mutual liberation. If, on the other hand, political power were to be equated with violence or the control of others, then political power would necessarily be an instrument of oppression.

The political realist, nevertheless, defines political power as "control over the minds and actions of other men"[7] and assumes that politics is the pursuit of this kind of power. The realist also justifies his identification of politics with power-as-control by asserting that striving for power is rooted in human nature. The implication is that oppression is an inevitable by-product of politics. Frederick Schuman indicates that "people with power relish the joy of commanding others to do their will."[8]

Political realism conflicts with a politics of liberation at three points. The first is in its assumption about human nature. The realist assumes that all human beings strive for power over others and do so throughout their lives as a part of their nature. In practice, however, many persons readily accept the leadership and even dominance of others. Many persons also discover that the process of maturing is one of learning to respect the rights of others and to cooperate with them in a give-and-take relationship, rather than to try to control them. In a relatively open society it is surprising how few people seek positions of power in the unions, clubs, churches, and other organizations to which they belong. Many refuse such opportunities for power even when they are offered. Even fewer run for public office or seek officer status in the armed forces. In the family, the primary social or political unit, the striving for power is often, if not usually, subordinated to cooperation and mutual support. In fact, the whole human experience demonstrates more reliance on cooperative activity in the building of houses, the gathering of food, and participation in other social and political organization than competition for power over colleagues, neighbors, and fellow citizens.

The second point of difference is in the question of whether politics is the pursuit of power to control or pursuit of influence or prestige. There is a vast difference between being an influential member of a Quaker meeting and being director of the F.B.I. or C.I.A., just as there is a difference between the prestige of being mayor of a city in which every decision is made by the city manager, and being chairman of the Board of I.T.T. Not all political goals are sought by or for the purpose of power according to the realist definition of power as control or domination.

The third point of difference is the realist assumption that politics is the pursuit of power for its own sake to be able to control other people. Many people, however, act as if politics is the pursuit of power to effect social change or to more effectively resist tyranny. Gandhi and Martin Luther King used power as a means of social change. Martin Niemöller's power in the German church was used to encourage church resistance to Hitler. If power is secondary to social change, it is nevertheless quite different from the realist idea of power for the sake of power.

The politics of liberation by definition involves the use of power for social change or the ending of oppression. It holds that power belongs to the people, that people can be organized in their own interest to oppose oppression, and that the cooperation of determined minorities can move or change governments in the direction of liberation.

Political power, when used by liberation movements, is necessarily rooted in large numbers of people. If it is impossible to win the support of at least tens of thousands of persons in a country the size of the United States, there is no popular consciousness of oppression and hence no basis for a significant liberation movement. Where there is mass support, however, the withdrawal of consent from a system or government is the exercise of tremendous power. For example, a boycott is the withdrawal of economic support from an industry, a chain store system, or anything else that depends on a volume of current income. In some Third World countries a mass boycott of a product made by a foreign concern could be coupled with a demand that twenty-five percent of the profits from that corporation's sales in that country be channeled into a cooperative that would give employment to persons earning less than three hundred dollars a year. Oil producing countries have successfully demanded such profit-sharing from the giant oil corporations by the threat to withhold oil production. People who are oppressed but who have purchasing power to withhold could use the same technique. The Montgomery, Alabama, bus boycott led by Martin Luther King resulted in the ending of segregated public intrastate transportation, for example.

The mobilization of purchasing power and its focused withdrawal from any product, coupled with demands for change, is far more effective than guns. Those who use violence are met by counterviolence, generally with the result that the question of injustice or oppression is no longer the primary focus in the public mind but is supplanted by a concern for public order or security. The fact of what will happen if a violent group takes over replaces any concern for the violence or oppression inherent in the system.

A second form of withdrawal of consent is one traditionally used by labor, the strike and, in exceptional situations, the general strike. This is so well known and so effective a form of power that it needs no further comment.

A third form of such withdrawal of consent is civil disobedience. It usually involves either massive refusal to obey a given law or disobedience by one or a few persons of conscience who dramatize the injustice of a specific law. In New York State a law that required people to go to designated underground shelters during civil defense drills was nullified when thousands of people massed in public squares and parks during such drills, protesting that they contributed to war hysteria. Gandhi led hundreds of thousands of Indians in disobedience to British laws as a method of ending colonialism. Various cases of civil disobedience in Latin America and elsewhere are cited in my earlier book, *Liberation Ethics.*[9]

The withdrawal of consent as a method of power can take many forms in addition to those listed above. They include sit-ins, the withholding by farmers of crops for market, fastings or hunger strikes in institutions such as schools and jails, the burning of draft cards, the "haunting" of public officials, refusal to pay taxes, and the like. The mere fact of the organization of a determined group of people to demand change often forces public officials to vote or act differently. As a result, pressure groups in a country like the United States tend to have more power between elections than does the voting public at election time. Voters generally tend to vote for persons or parties, whereas pressure groups focus on specific issues. They are capable of withholding or giving support to government officials in the form of votes. They can help finance campaigns or publicly analyze laws and spotlight the conduct of public officials. Lobbying itself is a combination of the furnishing of information to public officials, persuasion, offers of support, or subtle threats of withholding it. In other words, political power in its various forms inheres in numbers of people, in their cooperation, their commitment, and their tenacity.

Thus far we have been speaking descriptively or analytically about power. If we turn to the ethics of power, we must ask how power should be used, or perhaps what kind of power should be used. Stated another way, what kind of power is appropriate to our political purpose?

For this discussion we can classify power either as *enabling* or *disabling*. Ideas, actions, movements that actually liberate persons from oppression or addiction or from anything else that stands in the way of their being fully human and humane can be said to be enabling. Power that enables is life-giving; it means human dignity, freedom, hope.

The power to disable or destroy is what we generally speak of as the "power of evil." It confronts us in various forms. We can experience it subjectively as fear or guilt. Fear or guilt is disabling and robs us of our normal ability to accomplish a purpose. It was Samson's enervating guilt because he broke his vow not to cut his hair that robbed him of his power. There was no power in long hair as such. The feeling of being trapped or encircled, enslaved, or oppressed by overwhelming forces is also disabling.

But the power of evil is also a part of our environment. It exists in the economic systems that doom some people to poverty. It exists in all forms of totalitarian or military rule in which freedom of expression is not tolerated and persons in order to live must remain quiet about injustice or inequality. It exists in racial structures such as the segregation of blacks and Native Americans in the United States.

The power of evil is always either disabling or destructive. It may disable us so that we remain detached and uninvolved in the political struggle, or it may be manifest in a feeling of worthlessness or lack of dignity, or anxiety about our identity or place in the world. Such a feeling of worthlessness is generally marked by a sense of powerlessness and, therefore, loss of hope.

The power of evil is also evident in all methods that seek to destroy persons, such as war, violent revolution, philosophies that see one group's welfare as dependent on the destruction or disabling of another group.

When people speak of the power of love over against the power of evil, they refer to enabling and creative power as over against disabling guilt; it is the power of love that recognizes our worth and dignity.

In considering the ethics of power, it is always essential to examine at least four aspects of it: the goal, the motive, the method, and the consequences or probable consequences of any use of power. Any ethical use of power should automatically exclude utopian goals. By utopian goals I mean those that cannot be reached, such as a "classless society," or that cannot be realized with the approach to power that is available. It would not be possible, for example, to impose democracy on the world by war or achieve world government through the strengthening of national sovereignty.

Power can be used to impose the will of a group of oppressors on the large majority of the people, or it can be used to defend an existing system or structure of oppression. In either case it is an unethical use of power. Power ought to be used to eliminate oppression or, in other words, to serve rather than dominate people.

The motive for using power is also important. Sometimes a political party, whether capitalist or Communist, will propose a goal that, if accomplished, would raise the standard of living of the people, but the motive in doing so is to perpetuate the control of the government or the economy by the Party or the oligarchy, especially by the few party leaders who make the basic decisions. It would be naive for any group of people to expect unselfish motives from the leaders of any political or economic system. No group seeking political leadership can be expected to have wholly good motives. Nevertheless, it will always pretend to be functioning for the common good. It is the *people* whose task it is to evaluate the motives of their political and economic leaders so that they are not misled by the rhetoric or propaganda used. As nearly as possible the motivation should be one of liberation or, in other words, the meeting of the needs of all the people rather than the few who administer the systems of society.

The methods of power are extremely important because the means used always condition the result. Any means that disables rather than enables people is unlikely to produce a more humane society. A former Communist leader, Milovan Djilas, who was vice-President of Yugoslavia, wrote:

> Throughout history there have been no ideal ends which were attained with nonideal inhumane means, just as there has been no free society which was built by slaves. Nothing so well reveals the reality and greatness of ends as the methods used to attain them.
>
> If the end must be used to condone the means, then there is something in the end itself, in its reality, which is not worthy. That which really blesses the end, which justifies the efforts and sacrifices for it, is the means; their constant perfection, humanness, increasing freedom.[10]

If a choice has to be made between ends and means, we can say that the means are always more important than the goal. Just as the road taken determines the destination you reach, so the methods of power determine whether the end result will be domination or liberation. Destructive or disabling methods necessarily reveal that those using them view human life as cheap. Methods that treat human life as important are likely to lead to social structures that respect personality. Djilas adds:

> No regime in history which was democratic—or relatively democratic while it lasted—was predominantly established on the aspiration for ideal ends, but rather on the small everyday

means in sight. Along with this, each such regime achieved, more or less spontaneously, great ends. On the other hand, every despotism tried to justify itself by its ideal aims. Not a single one achieved great ends."[11]

The fourth aspect of the ethics of power is to examine the consequences or probable consequences of any particular approach to power. Any party, class, race, or nation that relies on violence to achieve its social goals is likely to maintain and perpetuate them by violence. The historical record reveals that the violence of the system of racial segregation is a consequence of the violence of human slavery, the violent slave trade, and the war between the states. The colonialism and imperialism of the West are related directly to the war system. The totalitarianism of Communism is related to violent revolution and a party whose whole existence and purpose originated in conspiracy to use violence.

The consequences of violent forms of power are generally destructive and disabling, so that it is possible to say "the more violence, the less liberation." The liberation approach to power, on the other hand, is based on serving rather than ruling, on nonviolence rather than violence, on conflict with rather than acquiescence to oppression, and on the building of communities of cooperation among the oppressed.

One of the great virtues of nonviolent power is that its chief use is the nullification of oppressive power. It can bring down governments or systems, but it is not a method that a small elite can use to maintain itself in power. The key factors in nonviolence are the withdrawal of support from a particular establishment or system and the acceptance of suffering rather than its infliction. These are directly contrary to the will to power over others and the establishment of institutions of dominance.

In one sense the conflict in the world is between those who imagine God as infinite power and want to put themselves in God's place to exercise power over others, and those who understand God as a representative or spokesperson of the oppressed, a servant of the people, whose power is limited by those who must be persuaded.

The politics of liberation identifies itself with this latter concept of God. Its aim is not simply negating the power of the oppressors, but creating new power among the oppressed that can be shared with all. The aim is the liberation of both the oppressed and the oppressor to a new way of thinking and acting.

The old way of thinking and a new way of thinking refer to ideologies, the way people have been conditioned by their social and political environment. It is essential, therefore, to examine the impact of ideology on social change.

6

POLITICS AND IDEOLOGY

In an imaginary country a group of one hundred wealthy families owned or controlled seventy-five percent of all the land, industry, and money. The other twenty-five percent was owned by the other hundred million people, one third of whom lived in very poor houses and had barely enough to eat. They didn't revolt against the hundred wealthy families because they had a common belief that anyone could become rich by working hard enough, saving money, and competing successfully with fellow citizens. Occasionally some poor person actually did get rich. That person's picture and story of success were printed in the newspapers the rich families owned. But none of the hundred wealthy families ever became poor. This system was called the "free enterprise system" because all citizens were free to work hard, earn money, and invest money wherever they wanted. The poor were free to criticize the rich and could even vote to elect people who had enough money to run for office. So they felt they had a share in running the government.

In another country there were no rich people because they had a different system of government. The government owned all the land and all industry, so everyone shared in the ownership. The government was run by a political party whose leaders made all the important economic and political decisions. The leaders decided where people should work, how much money each person could earn, and even where and how they should live. Their leaders, because they had more responsibility, were paid more money, lived in better houses, had several cars, and sent their children to special schools. Compared with most of the people in the country these leaders, who numbered several hundred, were rich and powerful. But no one called them rich, because they didn't own the land and industry; they only controlled it. No criticism of these leaders or of the government was allowed. The leaders published quotations from one or two top leaders who set forth the correct way of thinking and acting. Critics who deviated from the correct line were pressured to conform. If they did not admit their errors, they were put in mental hospitals and examined for insanity. This examination might take as long as several years. This system was called "communist" because everything was collectively owned and the party leaders were dictators only in the common interest of all the workers—and of course everyone was a worker.

Each of these countries had programs to convince people in other countries as well as their own that its system was better for the people. They called the other countries names, such as "imperialist" or "totalitarian." Each made the people pay taxes to maintain armies to protect their land and their way of life. Each country's common set of beliefs, which we can call its ideology, was set forth as the truth and was perpetuated by the newspapers, TV, the schools, and speeches by governments leaders. These leaders had more to gain by acceptance of these beliefs than did the people. Each country was ruled by an elite whose position, wealth, authority, and power depended on the people's acceptance of these beliefs.

These illustrations, of course, do not give us either a complete picture of ideology or its meaning. But they do suggest that people's thinking is shaped by the system in which people live and the propaganda of those who control the press, radio, TV, schools, and other means of communication.

Everyone engages in ideological thinking. In every country in the world thinking is conditioned by the political and economic systems in which people have been reared. As a result, liberation movements have been hampered or thwarted.

Karl Marx, however, is responsible for the idea that our social environment determines or conditions our thinking. He believed that humans must first of all produce the economic necessities of life, such as food, shelter, and clothing, before they engage in politics or become concerned about religion, art, and science. So he concluded that economic activity is more important than all other activity and, in fact, largely determines what people believe and do about politics, religion, and the like.

For example, if an economic system is built on human slavery, the legal structure will concern itself with such questions as the buying and selling of slaves and penalties for runaway slaves, including those who helped hide them. In a slave society, religion would not emphasize either liberation from oppression or social justice on earth, but rather a life after death where everyone would be free.

This means, according to Marx, that most of what we consciously think is really the product of the way our society is organized, and the way our society has taught us to think prevented us from thinking. From this comes the realization that we do not think objectively, but that our thinking is rationalization or false thinking.

Therefore one definition of ideology that a Marxist intellectual might give would be "a system of beliefs for which objective truth or reality is claimed but that actually reflects the vested interests of a ruling class or group." Ideology is thus associated chiefly with "false thinking."

The influence of Marx's statement that it is social structure that conditions our thinking extends far beyond Marxists. Most sociologists accept a theory of knowledge that holds that the society in which we are reared, its assumptions, and even the language and symbols with which we are taught to understand the world condition our ideas and beliefs. For example, the women's liberation movement is now explaining that our language conditions women to accept male domination. The word "man" has been used generically to include women. The word "chairman" has been used for the leader or head of an organization. And God has been understood as male by the use of the word "Father."

Peter Berger wrote:

> Society predefines for us that fundamental symbolic apparatus with which we grasp the world, order our experience and interpret our own existence. . . . Very few people . . . are in a position to reevaluate what has thus been imposed on them. They actually feel no need for reappraisal because the world view into which they have been socialized appears self-evident to them.[1]

The ideology with which we have been reared or that

society has predefined for us is always an obstacle to liberation. This was recognized in the biblical account of the liberation of the people of Israel. Yahweh, the God of Israel, would not let any of the people reared in slavery in Egypt enter the Promised Land because they had been mentally conditioned by slavery (Numbers 14:1-4, 20-24).

There is a similar recognition in one of Jesus' statements: "Unless a man be born again he cannot see the kingdom of God" (John 3:3).

In Matthew's account Jesus said the same thing in different words: "Unless you are converted and become as little children you shall not enter the kingdom of God" (Matthew 18:3). Little children are too young to have become captives of their society's ideology, too young to have developed vested interests in property, nationalism, war, racial, or other prejudices. Little children, in other words, have developed "no other gods," no other supreme loyalties, so that they are able to enter the kingdom of God, the liberated society, because, as Yahweh said, they have "no other gods before me" (Exodus 20:3).

The first step in the direction of liberation is to become conscious of our own vested interests, our own ideological commitments. The second step is to become aware that it is impossible to act or refrain from acting politically without ideological motivation. A third step is to examine ideologies, including our own, critically. This will not lead us away from all ideological thinking into pure or objective reason, but it may suggest standards by which to judge ideologies.

Neither Communist nor capitalist countries are culturally or ideologically monolithic. All complex societies, such as the U.S. and the U.S.S.R., are made up of different groups, some of which have a different interpretation of their culture from that of the mainstream. Ethnic groups and religious and scientific associations, for example, will often have some common ideology of their own that is not at all points identical with that of the existing political order. The fact that young people question their elders and traditional ways of doing things also suggests that cultures and ideologies are not monolithic and unchanging.

In a Western, capitalist country such as the United States, where there is freedom to hold different ideologies, a mainstream ideology emphasizes free enterprise, the right of private property, and certain other individual rights, but also emphasizes the duty of the individual to support the state and the military. Since the U.S. is not a totalitarian state, it is composed of many different groups that openly advocate their respective ideologies. There are organizations with an antiwar or anticapitalist analysis of society. They not only propagandize against the mainstream ideology but for a short time may prevail against it at one or more points, as happened in the growing resistance to the war in Vietnam.

There are so many ideologies that a more inclusive definition than that given by Marxists is necessary. Ideology is an idealized or in some cases absolutized program or philosophy that serves some political or social structure or goal. The goal is in turn used to legitimize the program or philosophy. Lenin gave us an illustration of what we mean by "absolutized." He said, "From that philosophy of Marxism, poured from a single chunk of steel, you cannot withdraw one fundamental premise or one essential piece without departing from objective truth and falling into the arms of the bourgeois-reactionary lie."

Western capitalism idealizes individualism with its stress on initiative, hard work, and thrift, together with a philosophy of competition. Success is determined by the accumulation of private capital. It is not opposed to religion as is Communism, but it nevertheless tends to nullify the deepest insights of the Jewish and Christian faiths. It does not deny the existence of a God of love but makes competition and material success the ground of our being rather than love or cooperation. In practice the ideology of private enterprise is a camouflage for the monopoly capitalism of the large, American-based, multinational corporations that dominate the world economy. The "free world" is an euphemism for the countries that are open to U.S.-based corporations, even though many of these nations are dictatorships.

It is even likely that each political and economic system is so interwoven with nationalism that much of the dynamic or drive of each system comes out of its identification with patriotism and nationalism. So capitalism is tied to the American national interest, as Communism is to Soviet or Chinese interests.

We can classify ideologies in the following ways:

1. There are ideologies that take a part of the human world, such as a race or a nation, and idealize its way of life or political program. The Nazi Party with its emphasis on nationalism and racial superiority illustrates this group, as does the Ku Klux Klan. All ideologies of racial superiority, nationalism, and cultural imperialism would be included in this category.

2. There are ideologies that take a part of the human experience, such as a political or economic system, and idealize it into a way of life or set it up as a total system through which all of history and reality are interpreted. This group includes capitalism, Communism, Marxism, and Maoism. It would not include those forms of democratic socialism such as Fabian socialism that do not view themselves as ideal or absolute formulations, but are simply alternatives to capitalism or Communism.

3. There are ideologies that idealize or absolutize a future existence or future society in such a way as to validate the existing order. In this category would fall all those who accept the existing order until God is ready to usher in his kingdom. Some forms of Protestant fundamentalism, in particular, tend to have no concern for changing the social order as such. They tend to view morality as individualistic. They emphasize the sins of sex or drunkenness but do not concern themselves with the larger sins of militarism, war, capitalism, and imperialism, which exploit entire populations. Therefore, writes Peter Berger, by concentrating "attention on those areas of conduct that are irrelevant to the maintenance of the social system," the fundamentalist "diverts attention from those areas where ethical inspection would create tension for the smooth operation of the system. In other words, Protestant fundamentalism is ideologically functional in maintaining the social system. . . ."[2]

4. Another form of ideology is a relativism that seeks to avoid commitment to any program of social change by advocating open-mindedness on everything. It thus tends to validate the status quo. In some respects "situation ethics" is a form of ideology, even though it claims to reject all ideology so as to be able to let love determine conduct in each specific situation. The author of the book *Situation Ethics*, Joseph Fletcher, maintains that a situationist cannot take a principled stand

against all war, because such a stand would be ideological.[3] If you cannot reject all war because that would be ideological, and instead must decide, when each war comes, whether it is a just or unjust war, you necessarily have to support the war system so you can participate in it if it seems to you to be just. This means support of the military-industrial complex or whatever it is that does the planning and preparing for war.

5. There is a fifth form of ideology that idealizes or absolutizes an organization or its structures or the pronouncements of its leader as coming from God and therefore not subject to criticism or change. When the leader makes a statement on faith or morals, however timely at the moment, its change in the light of new understanding would reflect on the leadership principle or the leader's perception of revelation. Thus it would undermine the authority of the church or cult. Whenever a church accepts and consecrates human judgments and values, whether a philosophical system or an ancient cosmology or cultural views of sex or race or male leadership it tends to look to the past or have a reactionary bias.

There is, of course, more in the faith of such churches than ideology. The point, however, is not to indict churches but to indicate that churches are not immune from the ideological temptation, and that churches as well as parties succumb to ideology.

6. There is a sixth form of ideology that idealizes or absolutizes a method of settling disputes or achieving social change. The idea that "power grows out of the barrel of a gun," that revolution has to be violent, that force or violence is the only language that everyone understands, or that the outcome of human history is finally determined by war, assumes that ultimate power and hence meaning are bound up with one form of coercion, the ability to intimidate and destroy. Violence becomes the decisive factor in human affairs, not because this is necessarily so, but because it is believed to be so.

7. There are also ideologies of social change such as those of the various liberation movements. These include women's liberation, black liberation, and comparable movements among Native Americans, Hispanics, and Third World countries. These do not necessarily absolutize their movements, but they often idealize their groups in order to build dignity and solidari-

ty. This is evident in slogans such as "black is beautiful" or in Third World nationalist emphases. Such groups would probably regard ideology as a system of thought in the light of which society and its goals are critically analyzed in the interest of the political and economic restructuring of society.

There are important values in ideologies of social change. Anyone who seeks planned social change must develop a strategy for change. Strategy presupposes some theory of a better society as well as proximate goals that lead toward it. In this respect an ideology that combines a theory of society with realizable goals and a strategy for achieving those goals is actually a guide or standard for political action. There is thus a basis for evaluating both past and proposed actions to see whether they are in harmony with the ideology.

A second major value of ideology lies in its vary nature. Since each ideology asserts or implies that it has the ideal or final answer, it finds it necessary to analyze and expose other ideologies that also claim to have the final answer. Ideologies of social change exist to question and oppose ideologies of the status quo and vice versa, but even ideologies of social change oppose and expose each other. Ideologies therefore perform the valuable service of unmasking the pretensions and exposing the contradictions in rival ideologies. The democratic socialists expose the contradictions in the ideologies of the various totalitarian Communists, and the Communists in turn unmask the false claims and weaknesses of capitalism. The various Communist parties attack each other as "revisionist" because they depart from the "pure doctrine" held by the attacking group.

A third value in ideology is that it provides a system of beliefs around which believers may be organized and mobilized for political action. Ideology thus differs from philosophy in that it is more than an explanation of the world. Its point, as Karl Marx observed, is to change the world.

Ideologies also avoid the "situation ethics" approach of unplanned activity that simply reacts to a given situation from "good motives." The "situation ethics" approach tends to become a chiefly momentary witness without commitment to a social or political goal and hence without continuing work toward that goal.

Ideologies of social change, even when they specifically deny the existence of any transcendent force or power, nevertheless serve a purpose beyond their own party or other interests. All systems of society and all societies fall short of the standards of genuine liberation. They are, therefore, unstable and carry within them the contradiction or seeds of their own destruction. Ideologies perform the useful purpose of analyzing in political language the evils of a given society and holding aloft the necessity of a fundamental transformation of society, which of course is the definition of revolution. Ideologies of social change not only challenge the inequalities and injustices of the status quo, but they also attack the justification of the status quo and the beliefs of those who want to preserve it. Since the name of God is frequently used by those who like things the way they are, ideologies of social change also force people to reexamine their understanding of loyalty to God.

Ideologies, on the other hand, are not the whole truth about human life or any society or system. All ideology is related to the Christian doctrine of original sin. In the context of a theology of politics, original sin is the common experience of seeing all things from our own point of view, as if we are each the center of the universe. Our ideologies and political opinions are shaped by our personal, class, religious, racial, or national interests. Then we deceive ourselves by believing that they are really the result of rational or objective thinking.

All ideology is human-centered thinking and hence finite. We are unable to think comprehensively or in terms of the whole truth about life. It is, therefore, essential to have a healthy skepticism about ideological claims to total truth.

Unfortunately, governments and other powerful interests are not willing to educate people to engage in critical thinking or look at the world as a universal family. They encourage partisan thinking and condition people through the school system, the media, and the statements of government leaders to respond to events from the national interest.

One of the conditioning influences on Americans is "civil religion." It can be described as a blend of references to God by the Founding Fathers and other leading public figures with the nationalist idea of Americans as God's chosen people and America as the Promised Land. Civil religion is embodied in the idea that, just as the Israelites left slavery in Egypt to enter the Promised Land that was flowing with milk and honey, so our forefathers left the tyranny of Europe to come to a land of hope filled with all that was needed for a good life.

One of the important doctrines of the civil religion that has become a part of the American ideology comes from the Declaration of Independence: " . . . all men are created equal" and "they are endowed by their Creator with certain inalienable rights. . . . " That equality has never been implemented in the United States for minorities, women, or the poor. Yet millions of Americans believe that the United States represents equality as well as freedom.

A second aspect of American civil religion is the creation of myths about certain Presidents or political leaders. Abraham Lincoln has become almost a religious figure. Lincoln's law partner, Herndon, is sometimes quoted as saying that Lincoln was "the noblest and loveliest character since Jesus Christ. . . . " Such statements are based on the assumption that Lincoln freed the slaves. His emancipation proclamation, however, was wartime strategy. It freed slaves only in the states that had seceded and therefore didn't free them at all. Lincoln specifically did not proclaim freedom for slaves in the border states that stayed with the North.

A third criticism of civil religion is its intimate relation to war. A religious mythology has been woven around the Civil War and Abraham Lincoln. The Battle Hymn of the Republic, which is sung in schools and churches throughout the country, sees in the marching of the Union soldiers "the glory of the coming of the Lord." There are lines in this hymn that seem to carry over into every war, such as "he died to make men holy, let us die to make men free." In actuality, men go to war not to die but to make the enemy die. It takes a heavy ideological imagination to equate the Christian idea of unarmed sacrifice on a cross with the idea of soldiers dying on a battlefield while trying to kill their fellow Americans in a civil war. Yet that is part of the American ideology.

The American civil religion has no doctrine of peace, just as American nationalism and competitive capitalism have no doctrine of peace. The ideological nature of civil religion is evident in its use as a support for the American military power position and its extension around the world.

President Roosevelt used civil religion as the basis for his doctrine of unconditional surrender in the Second World War. In his message to Congress June 6, 1942, he said:

> We are fighting as our fathers have fought, to uphold the doctrine that all men are equal in the sight of God. Those on the other side are striving to destroy this deep belief and to create a world in their own image. . . . No compromise can end that conflict. There never has been—there never can be—successful compromise between good and evil. Only total victory can reward the champions of tolerance and decency, and freedom, and faith.

President Reagan used civil religion on March 8, 1983, to sell his nuclear war program. He identified the United States as the symbol of goodness and the Soviet Union as the symbol and "focus of evil in the modern world."

This idea that the United States represents the forces of good is linked to the idea that the U.S. is the chief defender of freedom in the world and the leader of the "free world." Freedom is something that is supposedly guaranteed in the Bill of Rights of the Constitution, yet it is forever under attack by those sworn to uphold it as well as by other powerful economic and institutional interests. For the government, business, and millions of Americans, freedom is chiefly understood as free enterprise, which is a synonym for capitalism. The "free world" is not defined by human rights but is composed of those nations that are committed to free enterprise even when they are ruled by dictators.

When powerful interests identify freedom with capitalism, they define the enemy of freedom as Communism, even though the threat to American capitalism in Latin America may be coming entirely from non-Communists. Freedom, therefore, is increasingly identified with anti-Communism rather than with a positive expression of civil liberty. Likewise the enemies of capitalism or imperialism are assumed to be friendly to Communism or led by Communists.

The mere allegation or accusation by high government officials that another government or its leaders are "leftists" is sufficient justification for the overthrow of that government, or interference with elections or revolutionary change. A case in point was the U.S. decision to intervene in the Dominican Republic to unseat the elected President Juan Bosch, a non-Communist, and revise certain articles of their constitution that prohibited large land holdings and restricted the rights of foreigners to acquire Dominican land.

President Lyndon B. Johnson cloaked the subsequent U.S. invasion of the Dominican Republic with rhetoric about freedom. He said:

> Over the years of our history our forces have gone forth into many lands, but always they returned when they were no longer needed. For the purpose of America is never to suppress liberty, but always to save it. The purpose of America is never to take freedom, but always to return it, and never to break peace but to bolster it, and never seize land but always to save lives.
>
> One month ago it became my duty to send our Marines into the Dominican Republic, and I sent them for these same ends.[4]

A politics of liberation necessarily has to oppose the ideology of civil religion and the ideology that uses freedom to justify intervention in other countries to preserve imperialism or the status quo. Liberation is always opposed to the control of politics or the economy by an elitist group. Such groups are more concerned with their own landholdings, their own profits, and their own position of dominance than they are with equality or freedom or justice.

A politics of liberation is not free from ideology, because it cannot be neutral or objective about oppression. It must be consciously on the side of the oppressed. Yet, insofar as its goal is the liberation of every living person and its method is one of respect for everyone including adversaries, it is closer to the deep ethical insights of religion than it is to the traditions and culture of any nation, race, or class. When liberation movements are nonviolent, their struggle against oppression is in practice directed against all ideologies that seek to replace existing structures of domination with their own domination. Political action that renounces governmental and economic power in the interest of an inclusive or universal liberation minimizes loyalties to such interests as nation, race, party, class, and economic systems, which are the essence of most ideologies.

Political action that renounces governmental and economic power in the interest of an inclusive or universal liberation minimizes loyalties to such interests as nation, race, party, class, and economic systems, which are the essence of most ideologies.

Judaism and Christianity have a way of dealing with ideology by commitment to a more inclusive truth than political and economic systems embody. The commandment, "You shall have no other gods before me," which is the assertion of the sovereignty of God, is a way of relativizing all human claims to loyalty. A commitment to the kingdom of God keeps one from other total claims such as nationalism, capitalism, and militarism.

Such a commitment, however, does not mean that individuals are free from self or class or national interest. It does mean that they have a vision or standard by which to measure and evaluate such claims. They also have a biblical context in which the God of Moses, Isaiah, Amos, Jeremiah, and Jesus is on the side of the poor and oppressed.

It is also possible to say that Christian faith is built around the conviction that the future or the goal of history has already been revealed, so that ideologies of the future have been anticipated in the kingdom of God.

If, however, commitment to the kingdom of God is only verbal, an excuse for not engaging in the struggle against poverty, nationalism, militarism, and other forms of evil, it also is ideological in nature. Truth is not abstract in the sense that one can take refuge in the kingdom of God by claiming that it is true and involvement in anything short of it is false. In one sense there is no such thing as truth; there is only the pursuit of it. One knows the truth only by doing the truth. If nationalism, racism, and war are alien to the kingdom of God, one participates in the kingdom by political action against these evils. Silence gives consent. Those who proclaim the kingdom or preach love in our kind of society can avoid conflict with these evils only by engaging in hypocrisy.

7

THE ROOTS OF LIBERATION

Freedom is an idea about which people feel strongly. Yet there is little agreement on its meaning. For some people freedom is an individual matter, in that each person must have rights over against society, especially against government. Freedom thus depends on the limitation of arbitrary power. This is in general the position of political liberalism.

Others believe that freedom requires opportunities as well as rights: the opportunity to work and have a living wage, medical care, decent housing, and a good education. This is the emphasis of democratic socialism as well as of some modern political liberals.

There is also an understanding of freedom that is social rather than individual and that holds that persons are free only when living in an ideal society in which everyone is treated with an approximate equality. This is the position of Communism.

Freedom has also been interpreted as independence, the complete absence of parental restraints, or white or male or colonial domination. This is the emphasis of anticolonial movements and to some degree black and women's liberation, though these latter are more concerned with equality than mere independence.

Still another point of view is that freedom requires pluralism or as wide a range of choices politically, economically, and culturally as possible. This is a position held in Western democracies and is larely due to the heritage of the Renaissance and Reformation.

There is still another understanding of freedom, which is associated with the Judeo-Christian tradition, modern science, and Marxism. It holds that there are forces or factors in the world that are beyond our control that limit or condition our options. The scientist Herbert J. Muller wrote that collective behavior and therefore human history are governed by impersonal forces beyond human control. We have grown much more aware of the deep, involuntary processes of social change, the unintended results of all social and political action. Nobody planned the Industrial Revolution, for instance. . . . [1]

From this point of view freedom is not rebellion against these forces, whether they are called God, or the sum total of matter in motion, or that which is given to us in the nature of the world. Rather, freedom is an attempt to discern the nature of the world, to live in harmony with it rather than fight it. This is the traditional Jewish-Christian approach.

A more recent Christian interpretation of human freedom is that God is not a king or dictator humans must obey, but a partner or leader or parent who is fully committed to liberation and the right of difference. Those who hold to this interpretation think of God as completely free being, or freedom, just as Gandhi called God "truth" and Jesus used the term "love." This is another way of saying that the purpose of existence is liberation. But it is also a way of saying that freedom cannot be achieved apart from the free decisions of human beings. If freedom is given to us in the very nature of life, so that we are never finally content with any form of slavery or imperialism, then freedom would be as much a ground of our being as love. Freedom, however, is not static, as "ground of being" implies, but a dynamic concept in which each person's ability to make choices and participate in group decisions must be taken into account. Whatever else may be said of God, the essence of divinity includes freedom. This means that God must take account of human purposes and actions, quite as much as humans are influenced by the free actions of their fellows. The Christian God is never a neutral or philosophical concept, but one who makes a claim on those who work with him. The claim of God as freedom is evident in our drive for liberation from whatever it is that enslaves or oppresses.

The roots of liberation are found in a number of the above theories of freedom. Political liberalism, for example, has made an enormous contribution to human freedom. Liberalism is a product of Greek and Christian thought that asserted the basic rationality of persons, their intrinsic moral worth, and the spiritual equality of individuals. These ideas came through the natural law of the medieval church to the first liberals, who accepted them without the church's theological presuppositions. Liberalism is thus responsible for the idea of the inalienable natural rights that each individual has. These individual rights to privacy, free speech, free association, and freedom of religion that are imbedded in the American Bill of Rights, together with majority rule and minority representation and an independent judiciary, are among the key aspects of Western democracy. The variety of choices that are evident in pluralism are a by-product of freedom of association, freedom of religion, and free speech.

The chief value in liberalism is the idea that persons must not be restricted only to political relationships. The individual has economic, religious, cultural, and other personal interests to express as well.

There are, however, a number of criticisms of liberalism. One is that it made individual freedom an end in itself and did not include the whole area of community responsibility. The result is that individual free enterprise wasted natural resources, marred the countryside, and disregarded the needs of others, thus restricting the liberties of millions of people. This raises the question whether individuals can be liberated apart from a responsible and liberated community.

A second major criticism is that liberalism provides for formal political and legal equality of persons, but in practice maintains an economic inequality that nullifies for many people their equality before the law. The costliness of running for office or hiring a lawyer for civil suits or defense against criminal charges gives immense advantages to those who are rich.

Another criticism is that the divorce of liberalism from its theological foundations led to a greater reliance upon positive or statutory law and less upon individual rights of conscience. Freedom depended more on due process of law adopted and enforced according to authorized procedure than on the idea that law had to stand the test of justice. John Hallowell points to the "great difference between freedom from unjust compulsion and freedom from illegal compulsion." The result is that "freedom from illegal compulsion means, then, for all practical purposes, no more than freedom to do whatever the state has not yet forbidden."[2] The American Civil Liberties Union, which exemplifies political liberalism, is in constant litigation to preserve the inalienable rights of the individual in the United States, but does not, for example, deal with such unjust statutes as the Social Security law, which taxes the poor very heavily and the rich very lightly, or with economic inequality as such, or with community responsibility.

The Marxist-Leninist-Maoist approach holds that liberation from oppression means both the ending of capitalism and living in Communist society. Freedom is by definition identical with a classless society that will have in it no exploitation by private economic interests and no state action against individuals. The state, according to Communist theory, is expected to wither away. Prior to the achievement of a worldwide classless society, no Communist society can be free because of danger from external and internal enemies. Freedom for Communists, in other words, must be limited indefinitely for the sake of ultimate freedom, however far away that may be. Similarly, Communists believe freedom must be limited for non-Communist societies. Adam Schaff, the Polish-Marxist philosopher, wrote:

> As long as there are enemies of freedom, as long as they can fight effectively, so long will it be necessary to strive to limit their freedom. . . . This is why socialist humanism advocates limiting freedom as much as is necessary for the sake of freedom.[3]

Freedom within any Communist society, then, is limited to choices of action that are permitted by those in charge of the Communist Party. This, in effect, means those situations in which there are several possible courses of action, no one of which has been chosen by the Central Committee of the Party or its executive group as the only acceptable one.

Marxists also believe that the individual is socially conditioned from birth and therefore can never be really free from external forces. Persons are not able to shape social processes in any way they want, but are subject to historical development. There "are objective laws which regulate events in such a way that the individual must fit into the way events are moving."[4]

The postponement of freedom until the classless society arrives is a way of justifying dictatorship for the long term, because the classless society is a theory with no evidence to support it. The main weakness of utopian thinking such as the idea of the classless society is that the Communists have been unable to analyze either the conditions under which such a society could be achieved or the methods for achieving it. In fact, the function of proposing a perfect society involves both criticism of the existing society and the provision of a series of steps for the transformation of the present system.

This inability to plan for a classless society does not mean that nations ruled by a Communist party are all the same or that there is no evolution toward greater freedom. The *Wall Street Journal* of March 26, 1982, described "the newest and most capitalistic twist in Hungary's liberal socialism." This included laws that "allow aspiring businessmen for the first time to form small private moneymaking companies," and an "economic strategy of loosening central controls and turning more to market forces."

The deputy finance minister of Hungary, Miklos Villaryi, said, "We need a smooth international climate to continue our economic strategy." The key to any significant economic or political change toward more freedom depends on an international climate in which Communist nations do not have their backs to the wall economically or feel threatened militarily. Yugoslavia, which has gone further than Hungary, had that kind of security and was also able to develop what the *Wall Street Journal* called "more normal economic relations with the West."

It is a mistake to assume that Communism is identical with totalitarianism. All societies evolve and are responsive to external as well as internal conditions. Some proponents of Communism insist that eventually the people may be able to participate in free elections. Nations such as Yugoslavia, Hungary, or Czechoslavakia seem more likely candidates for such a step than the Soviet Union.

In any event, one of the values of the Communist approach lies in its emphasis on the collective interest rather than in letting those who are affluent exploit natural and human resources for their own profit. Theoretically, consumer needs are to be met as needed. There is therefore no advertising to artificially induce the purchase of articles that are not needed. In practice, decisions have been made by the party hierarchy for what those few persons deem to be in the national interest. The result has been a denial of decision making by the people, except at the local level.

A third major approach to political liberation is that of democratic socialism. It attempts to combine the major values of liberal democracy with some form of public ownership of major industries, services, and natural resources such as the Fabians persuaded the United Kingdom to adopt at certain points. The classic definition of socialism is the collective or public ownership of the major means of production and distribution. Democratic socialism, therefore, need not involve government ownership, but can depend on national, regional, or local producers and consumers cooperatives such as exist in the United States in rural electrification associations and farm cooperatives. Such socialism maintains full civil liberties for the individual and provides all basic medical, legal, and educational services to everyone. Those who prefer private services have access to them as well. All socialist theory is indebted in some degree to the thought of Karl Marx, but democratic socialism is rooted much more in ethical concepts derived from the Jewish and Christian traditions of liberation.

The fourth and oldest major approach to liberation is that described in the Hebrew and Christian Scriptures. From this comes much of the inspiration and ethical thinking for liberation movements such as those of blacks, women, Africans, and Latin Americans. The idea that the proper goal of politics is liberation is clearly set forth in a variety of ways in the Hebrew and Christian Scriptures. One of these is Jewish-Christian mythology. By myth we mean the depicting of a truth in story form that could not be so readily understood in abstract statements. The myth of creation is intended to say that men and women were created in the image of God. In other words, they were created in a state of freedom from captivity or oppression. The myth of the "Fall of Man" symbolized their captivity to self-interest and the political, economic, and military interests that flow from a primary concern for self or the political extensions of oneself. The biblical position is that men and women can realize their full potential only through personal and political liberation, which occurs when they have become reoriented toward looking at the world and their fellow creatures from the viewpoint and concern of God. In other words, they are liberated from self-centeredness and from the political and economic structures that feed their personal and class interest.

God, as we have already indicated, is depicted throughout the Hebrew Scriptures as concerned with the liberation of human beings. For example, God took the initiative in asking Moses to lead the Israelite slaves out of their bondage in Egypt and to a Promised Land of freedom. Only those who had been born free could begin a free society. According to the story, God was aware of the way social systems condition people, for he would not let anyone born in slavery enter the Promised Land. The drama of this whole episode, which Jews celebrate each year in the Passover festival, is central to Judaism. It is a reminder of their freedom and the community to which they belong.

Our modern word "liberation" is the equivalent of the biblical word "redemption," which comes from a common Aramaic word meaning "to break or tear away." It is used to describe both political liberation and individual freedom. It is also used to signify rescue or deliverance. The word "deliverance," which comes via the French from the Latin words *de* (from) and *liberare* (to set free) is a synonym for "liberation." There are specific references in the Hebrew Scriptures to deliverance from captivity (Zechariah 10:8-10; Psalm 107:2) or from adversity (2 Samuel 4:9; 1 Kings 1:29; Psalm 25:22) or from oppression and violence (Psalm 72:14). The word "redemption" is also used to describe the money payments for the release of persons from slavery (Exodus 21:8; Leviticus 25:47-49).

The preoccupation of the Israelites with liberation is evident in numerous passages with respect to the freedom of slaves, although they lived in a world in which slavery was customary. Hebrew slaves were to be liberated following the sixth year of their purchase (Exodus 21:2-6; Deuteronomy 15:12-18). Their freedom was justified on the ground that all the people belonged to God (Leviticus 25:55). The release of Israelite slaves was considered a *restitutio in integrum*, which is the Latin phrase for amnesty, or the restoration of the structure of Israelite society as it had been divinely conceived in former times, when in the desert social equality and a brotherly practice had obtained.

"Liberation" in the Hebrew Scriptures means setting persons free from whatever it is that enslaves or oppresses them. It also means the fulfillment of what human existence ought to be. It is therefore not identical with the process of creating an independent political unit. When the people of Israel were led out of bondage in Egypt, something more than the creation of an independent tribal confederation took place. A community was created with accountability to God that also included responsibilities to its individual members. In turn, the members accepted certain responsibilities to the community and to each other. These, however, did not include the complete liberation of all Hebrews, since many things incompatible with freedom, including slavery and discrimination against women, were a part of their culture. Ancient Israel does not present us with a perfect model of a liberated community. It did, however, set goals and pointed the way to an ultimate liberation. The vision held by Isaiah (Isaiah 11:1-12) played such an important part in the Christian understanding of liberation. Isaiah not only wrote of his vision of a peaceable kingdom, but also called upon Israel "to loose the bonds of wickedness, to undo the heavy burdens, and to let the oppressed go free. . . " (Isaiah 58:6). Isaiah also spoke of liberation without the inflicting of violence, and of a servant who was oppressed to the death but nevertheless interceded for his oppressors (Isaiah 53).

The Christian concept of liberation begins with the idea that Jesus is the redeemer, the one who sets persons free. His own statement of purpose, according to the writer Luke, is that God called him "to proclaim release to the captives, recovery of sight to the blind, and to liberate those who are oppressed. . . " (Luke 4:18).

The church has unfortunately subordinated the political message of liberation in the New Testament to an emphasis on freedom from personal sin and guilt. Virtually all contemporary as well as past Christian thinking assumes that it is possible to be delivered or rescued from a "fallen" condition by being reborn a new person. The apostle Paul spoke of those who "have put off the old man with his deeds; and have put on the new man which is renewed in knowledge after the image of him that created him" (Colossians 3:9,10). Yet there can be no complete deliverance from original sin apart from a social rebirth or commitment to the kingdom of God.

The kingdom, as we suggested in chapter 2, refers not to a king and his subjects, but to a revolutionary political concept of a king who was a representative of the people and who was chosen from the people as a brother. He was to be a servant whose whole life is that of liberating people from poverty and "from oppression and violence." This necessarily involved taking the place of those who are arrested and punished by oppressors.

Jesus took this role of king as his own model. Apparently thousands of his followers understood him to be such a king. His approach was one of calling people to participate in a new movement identified with the kingdom of God. In this new Jewish proletarian movement, no one issued orders or ruled. The key to membership was service to those in need. Yet Jesus also challenged the authority of those in power. One of these challenges was a well-planned dramatic entry into Jerusalem. If it had happened today, it would have been called a demonstration. Instead of riding on a stallion, symbolic of military or governing leaders, he choose a donkey, symbolic of both his servanthood approach to liberation and his nonviolent stance. He was hailed by thousands of his followers as a "king that comes in the name of the Lord." Such a demonstration of his influence and the size of the crowds who hailed him must have had an impact on the power structure of the city.

Any understanding of Jesus' role as king and liberator necessarily involves a brief look at the events that culminated in his death and the continuing acceptance by his colleagues of his ongoing leadership. One of those events was his challenge to authority at the temple.

Everyone over twenty-one years of age was required to pay a half-shekel temple tax each year. Those from abroad who had other coins and those from Judea who needed the exact coin could get their money changed, at a profit to the money-changers. In addition, there were booths or concessions for the selling of sacrificial birds and perhaps animals. The family of Annas, who was the high priest until he was succeeded by his son-in-law, Caiaphas, controlled the Temple and the trading area as well. So when Jesus overturned the tables full of coins and drove the money-changers and the pigeon-dealers out of the Temple, he was challenging the highest religious authority and his business interests. It was also a protest against nationalism, since commercial activity was taking place in the part of the Temple Gentiles could enter for worship. Jesus and his disciples used moral force such as we associate with Gandhi, since no one was armed except possibly with a whip improvised from cords. The only reference to a whip in the four accounts of this incident is by John, whose story is also the only one that refers to animals. Obviously a whip is needed to get cattle moving.

The context is one in which he "drove them all, both sheep and oxen, out of the Temple," then overturned the tables of coins and thereafter "told those who sold the pigeons 'Take these things away. . . . '" There is no evidence of anyone being injured, any violence, or the whip being used on persons. Rather this is akin to the moral force subsequently used by Gandhi but reinforced by large numbers of people exercising political power. Mark's account implies that Jesus had numbers on his side, because he and his disciples controlled the Temple area sufficiently that no one was allowed to carry any vessel or container through the Temple (Mark 11:16).

Two days before the Passover "the chief priests and the elders of the people gathered in the palace of the high priest, who was called Caiaphas, and took counsel together in order to arrest Jesus by stealth and kill him" (Matthew 26: 3,4). It is easy to indict the high priests for their scheming to get rid of Jesus. Their vested interests were at stake. But it is also possible that they were acting from what they considered patriotic motives. It was through the religion of Yahweh, centered in the Temple, that the Jewish people were held together. The Romans knew this and except in moments of crisis permitted conquered people to maintain the institutions that were important to them. Caiaphas and his father-in-law Annas were together exercising authority. They could not sanction another uprising like that of Judas Galilaeus because the Romans would not hesitate to kill any who were not involved, as well as those who were. Neither could they permit someone to establish a new religion that would displace them or divide the people. John reports that after one of Jesus' impressive miracles,

> The chief priests and the Pharisees gathered the council, and said, "What are we to do? For this man performs many signs. If we let him go on thus, everyone will believe in him and the Romans will come and destroy both our holy place and our nation." But one of them, Caiaphas, who was high priest that year, said to them, "You know nothing at all; you do not understand that it is expedient for you that one man should die for the people and that the whole nation should not perish. . . . " So from that day on they took counsel how to put him to death (John 11:47-53).

Caiaphas' argument was a powerful one because it appealed to religion and patriotism. John Erskine describes its import in these words:

> The Romans wished for friendly relations between themselves and the Jews, and to that end they wished through the high priests to keep the Jewish people in order. If, however, the people at some fatal moment should get out of hand, there was no doubt what the Romans would do. In crises of that kind they turned the soldiers on the people and killed them to the last man. Now if Jesus were to be the leader of his people, Caiaphas argued, he would soon prove unequal to the task of maintaining harmony among so many discordant elements. His was not a temperament to promote respectful accord. The high priests would be deposed and ruined when he undertook this control; when he failed in the attempt, the whole people would be destroyed.[5]

The high priests did not claim that Jesus was organizing an armed band. They were rather saying that he was becoming increasingly the leader of the people by virtue of his miracles and new political-religious teaching. Again and again the Gospels report that the Jewish power structure would have arrested Jesus except that the people would not have stood for it. The decision of the high priests and others from the Sanhedrin just before the Passover was to take "Jesus by stealth and kill him," but "not during the feast, lest there be a tumult among the people." Apparently Jesus was aware of this decision and of the necessity of any arrest being made at night when he was not surrounded by large groups of his followers. He had friends in the Sanhedrin. It is even possible that one of them warned him of Judas' offer to betray him. A crowd of armed men sent by the chief priests, which therefore probably included Temple guards, went to the garden of Gethsemane at night to arrest Jesus. Jesus himself is depicted in all of the Gospels as not resisting arrest. Neither did Jesus resist when one of the high priest's officers struck him during interrogation, or when he was struck and slapped at his trial before the Sanhedrin.

When he was taken before the Roman governor of Judea, Pontius Pilate, he startled Pilate by not protesting his innocence, as most persons do whether or not they are guilty. The charge made against him was one with a double meaning: that Jesus claimed to be the Messiah or king of the Jews. Such a charge had one meaning to the high priests—blasphemy—because of Jesus' interpretation of his relation to God. The meaning to a Roman governor was political—a possible threat to Roman rule, although the Gospels depict Pilate as not taking seriously Jesus' kingship. Jesus' own understanding of the word "king" was that of Isaiah —a brother and servant king who represented and spoke for the people as well as for God. Jesus could not have explained to a representative of the emperor that this was no threat to Rome, for his whole ministry was aimed at undermining all human loyalties. "Thou shalt have no other gods before me," whether nationalism, money, power, success. Caesar symbolized all of these. Pilate, however, according to the Gospels, believed Jesus was innocent but yielded to the pressure of the Jewish hierarchy to crucify him.

The most plausible explanation of Pilate's attitude relates to Roman politics. Pilate was probably named as prefect of Judea by Aelius Sejanus, who was prefect of the Praetorian Guard and handled the affairs of Tiberius in Rome while the emperor was away from that city. Sejanus was notoriously anti-Semitic and had taken various actions against Jews. Pilate had been tough with the Jews during his administration, apparently because of the known policy of Sejanus. Sejanus was ambitious and on his way toward becoming "de facto joint emperor and successor" to Tiberius. "But the Sejanian conspiracy was exposed and Sejanus himself executed on October 18, A.D. 31."[6]

Thereafter Tiberius abandoned his anti-Semitic policy and, according to Philo, ordered his procurators to go along with the customs of the Jews. Pilate had obviously received the orders from Tiberius and undoubtedly been wondering if he would be discharged or even destroyed along with others in the camp of Sejanus. Paul L. Maier writes:

> Now the vulnerable and defensive posture of Pontius Pilate on Good Friday makes immediate sense. . . . He could not tolerate a Jewish appeal to Rome in the case of one Jesus of Nazareth, since the complaint would undoubtedly be framed about the charge already presented at Pilate's tribunal: that Jesus had made treasonable claims to kingship. At a time when Tiberius was prosecuting adherents to Sejanus precisely under the rubric of *maiestas*—treason to state and emperor—the prosecution's threat in John 9:12 was masterfully barbed and weighted.[7]

The threat was sufficient: "If you release this man, you are not Caesar's friend; every one who makes himself a king sets himself against Caesar." Pilate apparently had no evidence of any action on Jesus' part against Rome, for that would have been a sufficient basis for action. But Pilate, in view of the political changes in Rome, was not prepared to risk his life or career for Jesus.

When Jesus was sentenced, he was scourged, taunted, and finally crucified. Crucifixion in this part of the empire involved the public exposure of the naked convict whose hands were nailed to a horizontal crossbar and whose feet were nailed to an upright post. Apparently the way in which Jesus stood trial and went to his death was convincing. Certainly it was unusual, if not unique, for a person while being crucified to say: "Father, forgive them. . . . " Mark asserts that the Roman centurion at the cross said: "Truly this man was the Son of God," while Luke adds that all the multitudes who assembled to see the sight, "when they saw what had taken place returned home beating their breasts" (Mark 15:39; Luke 23:47f.).

The various incidents in which Jesus confronted power reveal that he was primarily concerned with challenging established procedures or systems such as the law and legalism, corruption in the Temple, and the whole institutionalized conception that power lay in the ability to rule rather than serve. The conflict with those who defended the system was a strong and persistent one in which Jesus tried to undermine their authority without seeking to injure or kill them. That he opposed systems without seeking the injury of those involved is evident from his various relationships or encounters with tax collectors, Roman officers, temple guards, and others. Jesus not only rejected the use of violence against others but accepted it upon himself, in the conviction that liberation involved undeserved suffering for the enemy and all who were oppressed.

The early church, which was in a far better position than modern interpreters to understand what Jesus meant or intended, believed that the lifestyle of Jesus and his manner of dying meant victory. It was the way to liberation or to triumph over the powers that enslaved them. That is why they called him the Redeemer. It was first-century Christians who wrote the Epistles and the Gospels and who were responsible for the first interpretations or theologies by which the church understood itself and its mission. They saw the cross as the key to the problem of evil in the world. They were guided in this by Isaiah's "suffering servant" and therefore taught that suffering love is what redeems or frees everyone.

The cross as a means of redemption or liberation has been widely misunderstood because of the way some churchmen have tried to explain it. The word "ransom" for example, which is a synonym for redemption, means to deliver from any calamity or misfortune, however it is accomplished. It does not necessarily mean the payment of money or its equivalent, in the sense that the death on the cross was a price paid to someone. The idea of ransom, or the paying of a debt to appease the devil, or a price paid to persuade God, includes the idea that the suffering on the cross all by itself has redeemed those who believe in it, once and for all. This is very close to the superstitious idea that an animal sacrificed on an altar secures some blessing for the person to whom the animal belonged. This is the idea that liberation is something we can have given to us and thereafter enjoy. The cross is liberating once and for all only in the sense that there has now been demonstrated the only way real liberation can take place. Instead of being a *substitute* act it is a *representative* act in that no persons or group can be liberated unless they appropriate this "suffering service" for themselves. Suffering is a price required of anyone who persistently challenges injustice. But suffering is liberating only when accepted willingly without the retaliation that imposes a new form of oppression or injury on others. Suffering is not the appeasing of an angry God, for God is depicted in the New Testament as taking the initiative in sacrificial love (Romans 8:32; Galatians 1:4; 1 John 4:10). Similarly, liberation is not understood as individals delivering themselves from oppression. Rather, through an act of faith they understand that suffering service is the necessary way God liberates and helps persons to be liberated. Faith is depicted in the New Testament as accepting and following the lifestyle of Jesus. It is clearly stated, among other passages, in the following: "For hereunto were you called; because Christ also suffered for you, an example that you should follow in his steps: . . . who when he was reviled, reviled not again; when he suffered, threatened not . . . (1 Peter 2:21-23).

Early church members not only spoke and wrote in this vein, they acted in the same way. When Stephen was persecuted and then stoned to death, he forgave his murderers. One of them, Saul of Tarsus, was, through this act, liberated from being a persecutor consumed by hatred. He was in turn imprisoned, flogged, and persecuted. He also suffered in other ways during his work.

Nor was the work of the early church without political implications. In building a movement whose basis was contrary to the whole purpose of the Roman Empire, these people inevitably got into trouble. Acts 5 reports the arrest and imprisonment of "the apostles," including Peter. They escaped from prison, another act of civil disobedience. The early church did not believe that Jesus' life and death absolved them from participating in the process of liberation.

In trying to win others to his movement Jesus' followers developed a theology of political as well as personal liberation. They understood themselves to be part of a movement whose leader was in some mysterious way still alive and with them. After their initial feeling of defeat at the cross they came to realize that in all their conversation, thinking, and action Jesus was a continuing presence motivating and guiding them. The political impact of that presence was exemplary in that they set up a new center of loyalty parallel to that of the government, the church, that commanded their real allegiance. This was a revolutionary step because loyalty to the church meant a withdrawal of loyalty from the empire. They gave formal obedience to law when it was not contrary to their loyalty to Jesus and his kingdom. The political significance of the Resurrection lies in its evidence that death has no power over the genuinely free person. It cannot either as threat or actuality bend a free person to do the tyrant's will. The Resurrection is also a symbol of the fact that tyranny can do anything it wants to love and liberation, as it did at the cross, but if the crucified one still remains loving and free from any spirit of retaliation or revenge, it is evidence of the triumph of love over hate and freedom over oppression.

The Resurrection also suggests that political action that serves and liberates others, that does not injure or demean them, and that endures oppression will continue to have an impact on history even if it experiences defeat or persecution. Faith assumes that in a moral universe a good God welcomes and uses such action, rather than permits its obliteration.

This does not suggest that God is all-powerful in the sense that God can do anything. If that were the case, there would be no explanation for permitting the defeat of goodness and the success of evil. Power exists not only in God but in all creatures. Power is the ability to make choices and influence events and the decisions of others. God's power must be understood as rooted in love and freedom. Love presupposes freedom of response, not the manipulation of puppets. Love is voluntary and must be won rather than coerced or compelled. The power of evil is anything that expresses resistance to love and liberation. Political evil is evident in resistance to an inclusive, liberated community.

The Christian theory of political action presupposes a political process that does not culminate in a termination of history followed by some cataclysmically established kingdom. The process is a continuing one. This does not mean that humans cannot destroy the earth by nuclear war or other ecological damage. It does mean that God is not an absolute monarch but one who can be and is resisted. God is one who serves, whose power is rooted in freedom and love and in the nature of beings who need to love and be loved, and who need to be free and set free. The perversion of love and freedom and the attempt to dominate others are real. Therein lies the class struggle, and the clash of nations and other groups.

The fundamental conflict in our world is between oppression and liberation, violence and nonviolence, domination and cooperation. The church was clearly partisan in those conflicts until, under Constantine, it won its right to exist without persecution. It gradually became institutionalized and changed sides to become an ally of oppressive imperial and national governments. It came to endorse feudal, capitalist, and warmaking systems alike.

Nevertheless, Jewish and Christian concepts of liberation have had a profound impact on modern liberation movements. Among those movements that owe a debt to biblical ideas of liberation are those inspired or led by John Huss, William Wilberforce, Quakers who operated the Underground Railroad, American abolitionists, Keir Hardie (founder of the British Labor Party), Mohandas Gandhi, Chief Luthuli of South Africa, Martin Luther King, A. J. Muste of the Fellowship of Reconciliation, and the Latin American movement called "Priests of the Third World." In addition, Karl Marx, John Locke, James Madison, Thomas Jefferson, democratic socialists like Jean Juarez, the British Fabians, Eugene Debs, Norman Thomas, and contemporary black leaders in Africa and the United States were and are obviously influenced by the same tradition.

Except when the church has gotten trapped into taking itself too seriously as an institution exercising the power of Jesus on earth, instead of being his disciples, Christians as well as Jews have had a transcendent frame of reference or reality by which to judge their social, political, and economic experiences, including their programs of liberation. That transcendent reality cannot be captured by dogma but is experienced in persons and events. It cannot be captured by ideology or human vested interests. As former French Communist leader Roger Garaudy put it, the Christian faith "not only teaches us a negative theology that prevents us from saying that God is this or that and so enclosing him in a definition, but also provides us with a negative anthropology that prevents us from saying that man is this or that and so enclosing him in a definition."[8]

Just as there is no definition to enclose us, so there is no blueprint of the liberated or beloved community. The drama of history is not being played according to previously written lines.

The purpose of the kingdom of God is to remind the oppressed that they need not be enslaved by the politics of today. They can instead experience the politics of liberation. Millions of human beings—Jews, Christians, Marxists and others—can and will contribute to that liberation. It was Karl Marx and his followers who alerted Christians to the fact that they had "ceased to be a ferment in history" and had "retreated into the ghettos of heaven or eternity," that they were "content to explain the world instead of changing it," that they looked upon the "joyful news of the Gospel . . . as a ready-made truth rather than as a task to be accomplished."[9]

The future society is never achieved by defending the existing order. Nor is anything accomplished by anti-Communist societies with their numerous evidences of oppression. Prophetic religion calls us to look ahead and go beyond the past and the present to create a new and unpredictable social order that will capture the imagination and loyalty of Communists as well as non-Communists, Christians as well as non-Christians.

The politics of liberation does not envision a perfect society or a final goal. It is human destiny to live in a dynamic and ever-changing world, to have a divine discontent even with the good so long as it can be better. It is also human nature to be finite and therefore recognize that perfection is a process, not an achievable or definitive goal.

Liberation is in one sense a gift of God, a miracle to those afflicted with oppression and threatened by war or famine or racism or other forms of evil. But we do not receive it without participating in its achievement. God "does not save us from outside, as if giving us a present, but from within, since it is our deciding that saves us." In the New Testament miracles there is no magic. "Everything happens in the minds and wills of men. He doesn't say, 'I have saved you' as one might in fishing out a drowning man. He says 'your faith has saved you,' which . . . reminds us that the entire drama of God, without residue or exception is played out in our human lives."[10]

CONCLUSION

The traditional understanding of political action is that its goal is control of or participation in the control of government. Usually such control assumes a continuation of existing political, economic, and military systems and acceptance of the prevailing ideology. An alternative approach is to think of political action as deriving its meaning from the kind of society we want in the future. Henry David Thoreau in his *Essay on Civil Disobedience* wrote, "Let every man make known what kind of government would command his respect, and that will be one step toward obtaining it." This can also be stated in more ultimate terms: Politics should be shaped by our conviction about the purpose and goal of history. Plato, many centuries ago, said that in heaven there is a pattern for a perfect society and he who perceives it should live after the manner of that city, having nothing to do with any other. This is akin to the Christian idea that the vision of a future kingdom of God requires action now to realize that kind of society.

Is freedom or a free society the goal of history? Is it possible to imagine a society free from war, poverty, and racial, sexual, and other discrimination? The crucial question is not whether a perfectly free society is attainable but whether working toward an approximation of it is worth our commitment and energy. Can any black person be content in accepting a future in which racial segregation or discrimination is permanent? Can women resign themselves to a society in which rape, economic dependence on men, and other attributes of sexual discrimination are characteristic or usual? Can the world continue much longer under the shadow of nuclear war and the tremendous accompanying waste of human and natural resources in preparing for it? How long can humans pollute the land, water, and air if the earth is to survive and replenish itself?

Those committed to a politics of liberation do not define

politics as the art of the immediately possible but as the possibility of living, acting, organizing, and creating a public demand for a free society in which persons are respected and the future can be faced without fear. This means we do not have to engage in, or refrain from, running for political office in order to help create the conditions or support for the new society.

Matthew Arnold, who with his colleagues in England fought for many unpopular causes, captured something of this spirit. He wrote:

> We have not won our political battles, we have not carried our main points, we have not stopped our adversaries, advance, we have not marched victoriously with the modern world; but we have told silently upon the mind of the country, we have prepared currents of feeling which sap our adversaries' position when it seems gained, we have kept up our communications with the future.[1]

The purpose of political action, then, is not to get elected to office or achieve political power but to begin or continue the process of liberation, to help create support for a free society. There is a sense in which the question of achieving political power is the wrong question. We don't choose to be powerful or powerless. There is always a context in which we work. We don't decide, for example, when to deal the death blow to imperialism, racism, or war. We are not powerful in that sense because we cannot control either the various forces operating in history or the timing of genuine change. We can decide to add our own power and energy to those who are already committed to liberation. Instead of seeking control over history, we participate in creating the conditions in which the work of liberation moves forward cooperatively. Power, then, is not the control of other people via political office; it is working with them to help thrust forward the liberating purpose of history.

The first step in being a factor in the struggle for human freedom is to examine our own involvement in and acceptance of unfreedom or oppression. We cannot influence or persuade others if we are not persuaded ourselves. If our language, our symbols, our stories, our investments, the organizations to which we belong, the periodicals we read, and the way we spend our time and money do not reflect a deep concern for liberation, it is time for a change. Lord Byron in "The Prisoner of Chillon" has François Bonnevard conclude:

> My very chains and I grew friends. So much a long communion tends to make us what we are; even I regain'd my freedom with a sigh.[2]

"The real slavery of Israel in Egypt" according to Rabbi Hanakh of Alexandria, "was that they had learned to endure it." Insofar as we continue to accept the existing order and maintain our ideological support for it, we are not free. Freedom is more than the absence of restraint; it is also release for action. Our ability to realize freedom depends upon our awareness of being unique persons. Or, as Nietzsche put it, "Freedom is the capacity to become what we truly are." We cannot be an influence for liberation unless we internalize the free society we want to achieve.

Some people may not feel a need for freedom. They may live in a society whose ideology and actions they have never questioned because the society so constantly calls itself free or is relatively free in comparison with certain other societies. The anthropologist Franz Boas wrote that "A person who is in complete harmony with his culture feels free. He accepts voluntarily the demands made upon him." Therefore, Boas concludes, "the concept of freedom can develop only in those cases where there are conflicts between the individual and the cultures in which he lives."[3]

Conflict between individuals and their culture arises when they experience injustice to the point of resentment or resistance or when their conscience is aroused because of the suffering of others. When most Americans accept preparation for nuclear holocaust, it is evidence of a failure to imagine their own suffering in the event of war and hence any injustice to themselves. It is also evidence of a lack of conscience about the suffering of others. To some degree, also, it is evidence of a complete harmony with the prevailing ideology that it is better to destroy the Soviets even if most Americans die in the process than it is to negotiate a disarmament agreement or accept something less than number one status. Change, including a change to justice or peace, is impossible without a break with the prevailing ideology.

A second step in being a factor in the struggle for human freedom is to become more and more sensitive to the injustices, indignities, and inequalities that other people suffer. Many people do not know, either as friends or acquaintainces, Native Americans, Hispanics, blacks or people suffering from malnutrition, functional illiteracy, or other forms of deprivation. Without such knowledge or experience, which must be consciously chosen, consciences can only be sensitized by reading, drama, or other art forms that move one deeply, or by dialog with those already deeply aroused.

It is not easy to develop a conscience about the suffering of other persons in our society. Governments and corporations go to great lengths to keep people thinking of humans in abstract terms, such as "people on welfare," or "draft dodgers" or "leftists" or other names that stigmatize them so as to prejudice us against wanting to know them as the unique individuals they are. Governments and corporations don't want us to think of changing laws or power arrangments to accommodate persons. They expect persons to conform to the law and the prevailing ideology.

The insight of all ethical religion that every person is to be respected is essential to good politics. The further insight that freedom is the essential condition of moral life means that those who live in grinding poverty or experience the indignity of racism are not able to participate fully in their own destiny unless we assist them in the process of liberation.

A third step we can take is to resist and expose the devil theory of politics and slogans like "the lesser of two evils" that are designed to coerce us into taking a predetermined course instead of analyzing or thinking for ourselves. For centuries millions of people believed that the power of evil resided in a devil who thwarted God's purposes and was responsible for the countless misfortunes of people. The devil lives on today for many people in the form of Communism or in its chief home, the Soviet Union. As a result, the injustices in our own society are obscured for us by our preoccupation with the Soviet Union. If we don't sacrifice our standard of living through higher taxes, lower wages for police, fire, and teaching personnel in our cities, and fewer food stamps for the poor, and give the military-industrial complex everything it wants, the devil will nibble away at the Middle East, endanger the oil lifeline, invade Africa, or fortify Cuba.

The obsession with the Soviet Union permits super-patriotic groups and the government to cast doubts on the loyalty of anyone who questions the current devil theory. The great test of political orthodoxy for American nationalism is anti-Communism. Anti-Communism is also an excuse for continued oppression. Many people assume that any serious attack on militarism or capitalism, or any serious effort to deal with poverty, or any attempt to provide national health security for the poor is ipso facto playing into the hands of the devil.

Anti-Communism differs from ordinary opposition to Communism in that it tends to be an emotional and irrational reaction that is often the basis for stereotyping and scapegoating. One of the terrible things about it as a national mood is that anything, especially any reverse in U.S. fortunes internationally or any indigenous revolution, can be blamed on Communism or the Soviet Union. The devil is a convenient scapegoat. The charge is also used to stifle or dismiss healthy criticisms of the military-industrial complex and imperialism as well as other systems and thus rob all of us of the free flow of opinion.

A fourth step we can take is to work for more democratic participation by everyone in all the enterprises with which we are connected, including educational institutions, churches, labor unions, business enterprises, and civic organizations. For example, wherever possible workers and consumers should be encouraged to buy, manage, and operate small business firms.

In the East are the Vermont Asbestos Group with 175 workers, a Herkimer, New York, library furniture factory, and other similar worker-owned enterprises. The employees of the Chicago and Northwestern Railroad purchased it in 1972.[4] The output per hour of work tends to be higher in worker-owned enterprises. There is less absenteeism and fewer strikes, and energy savings of twenty percent are not uncommon.[5]

One way in which workers have come to own their own plants is through the assistance of the towns in which they are located when an outside corporate owner decides to close the plant. In some cases the town bought the plant and gradually sold it to the workers. Increasing the number of collectively or democratically owned and operated plants is one approach to the liberation of workers and communities.

Fifth, we can join or support minority movements whose goal is liberation. These may be pacifist or socialist groups or movements for the liberation of specific groups such as blacks, women, or Native Americans. In a highly organized society those who want to abolish war and liberate people from poverty or inequality have little power or influence apart from an organized group. If we are articulate, our volunteer services as speakers, writers, or organizers will be helpful. If we are inarticulate, the organization or movement can be our spokesperson.

Wherever possible we should, as Walter Brueggeman suggests, join in "the formation of an alternative community with an alternative consciousness . . . so that the dominant community may be criticized and finally dismantled." Brueggeman indicates that the real "purpose of the alternative community is to enable a new human beginning to be made"[6] and not simply to dismantle the prevailing ideology and systems of oppression.

Finally, we should also educate and persuade others to shift their emphasis away from a philosophy of competition and power over people to one of cooperation and service. This is not to negate power but to harness it to our purpose of liberation. Jesus rejected his third temptation because he was offered power for a purpose other than what he wanted to do. Should a journalist accept a position on a periodical whose policy is the defense of oppressive systems? Should political candidates compromise their deepest convictions in order to advance toward higher political office? Bertrand Russell described such a person in these words: "To advocate unsuccessfully what he wants seems to him more futile than to advocate successfully what he does not want." This raises questions about our participation in jobs, professions, or organizations that put us more or less inevitably on the side of oppression. It also means that no one can advocate liberation without the willingness to make sacrifices or experience defeat. There is no possibility of fundamental social change without the feeling of pain.

Yet politics is never strictly political. There is always a

moral element that, properly raised, can stop or change the best laid plans of corporate or governmental leaders. The discerning of that moral element is the task of everyone devoted to liberation. That moral element will obviously include resistance to anything that demeans or disables persons. It will also raise issues that colleagues, friends, and the general public cannot ignore without some wrestling with their own immediate position or ultimate commitment.

ENDNOTES

Chapter 1: THE POLITICS OF LIBERATION

1. *New York Times*, April 26, 1967.
2. Frantz Fanon, *The Wretched of the Earth* (New York: Grove Press, 1966), p. 207.
3. John M. Swomley, Jr., *Liberation Ethics* (New York: Macmillan, 1972), p. 2.
4. Mark 10:41.
5. Chester Bowles, *The New Dimensions of Peace* (New York: Harper and Brothers, 1955), pp. 149-50.
6. Swomley, *Liberation Ethics*, pp. 69, 203-205.

Chapter 2: THE ORIGIN AND NATURE OF GOVERNMENT

1. Franz Oppenheimer, *The State*, tr. Gitterman (New York: Vanguard Press, 1922), p. 68.
2. Robert M. MacIver, *The Web of Government* (New York: Macmillan, 1947), p. 22-3.
3. This is a summary of an analysis by Hans Walter Wolff, "Masters and Slaves," in *Interpretation*, XXVII (July 1978).

Chapter 3: CHRISTIAN THEORY OF GOVERNMENT

1. *The Political Christ* (Philadelphia: Westminster Press, 1973), pp. 41-43.
2. Frederick C. Grant, *The Gospel of the Kingdom* (New York: Macmillan, 1940), pp. 107, 108.
3. Ethelbert Stauffer, *Christ and the Caesars* (Philadelphia: Westminster Press, 1955), p. 128.
4. Ibid., pp. 124-126.
5. Ibid., p. 130.
6. Quoted in Spencer Kennard, Jr., *Render Unto God* (New York: Oxford University Press, 1950), p. 116.
7. Ibid., p. 123.
8. Kennard, p. 124.

9. R. H. Strachan, "The Gospel in the New Testament," *The Interpreter's Bible* (Nashville, Abingdon Press, 1951), 7:16.

10. John H. Yoder, *The Christian Witness to the State* (Newton, Kansas: Faith and Life Press, 1964), p. 75.

11. C. J. Cadoux, *The Early Church and the World* (Edinburg: T. and T. Clark, 1955), p. 47.

12. Stauffer, p. 175.

Chapter 4: POLITICAL REALM

1. The December 2, 1980, *New York Times* described the invasion of the offices of three peace groups in Chicago in 1967 by the Security Division of the Chicago Police Department's Intelligence Division. One of the police had a key to the offices because he had infiltrated the Chicago Peace Council and become its secretary. The other organizations were the Fellowship of Reconciliation and Women for Peace. The police took postage stamps, money, membership and contributor lists, typewriters, and other office equipment from the three organizations. The Chicago Police Department, with the help of about 850 informants, infiltrated and used electronic surveillance against more than 800 organizations, including the League of Women Voters, Parent Teacher Association, the American Jewish Congress, the World Council of Churches, and the NAACP. Reports were sent to the FBI and Army Intelligence; there was also daily contact with these groups.

2. *Los Angeles Times*, June 22, 1981.

3. Harold J. Laski, *Politics* (Philadelphia: J. B. Lippincott Co., 1931), p. 22.

4. Reinhold Niebuhr, *Christian Realism and Political Problems* (New York: Charles Scribner's Sons, 1953), p. 96.

5. *New York Times*, July 25, 1974.

6. Reinhold Niebuhr, *An Interpretation of Christian Ethics* (New York: Harpers, 1935), p. 89.

7. Sigmund Freud, "Dostoevsky and Patricide" in *Guilt:Man and Society*, ed. Roger W. Smith, (Garden City, New York: Doubleday and Company, 1971), p. 64.

8. *New York Times*, August 9, 1974.

Chapter 5: POLITICAL POWER

1. Karl Mannheim, *Man and Society in an Age of Reconstruction*, (New York: Harcourt Brace and Co., 1951), p. 167.
2. Chester Bowles, *The New Dimensions of Peace* (New York: Harper and Brothers, 1955), p. 16.
3. Erich Fromm, *Marx's Concept of Man* (New York: Frederick Ungar Publishing Co., 1961), p. 24.
4. Ashley Montagu, *Darwin, Competition and Cooperation* (New York: Henry Schuman, 1952), p. 67.
5. Ibid., p. 79.
6. Hans J. Morganthau, *Politics Among Nations*, 2nd ed. (New York: Alfred A. Knopf, 1959), p. 26.
7. Fredrick L. Schuman, *International Politics*, 3rd ed. (New York: McGraw-Hill, 1941), p. 261.
8. John M. Swomley, Jr., *Liberation Ethics* (New York: The Macmillan Co., 1972).
9. Milovan Djilas, *The New Class* (New York: Fredrick Praeger, 1957), p. 162.
10. Ibid.

Chapter 6: POLITICS AND IDEOLOGY

1. Peter Berger, *Invitation to Sociology: A Humanistic Perspective* (Garden City, New York: Doubleday, 1963), p. 117.
2. Ibid. p. 114.
3. Harvey Cox, ed. *The Situation Ethics Debate* (Philadelphia: Westminister Press, 1968), p. 263.
4. Statement of June 3, 1965, quoted in the U.S. Department of State Publication 7971 (Washington, D.C., 1965). Inter-American Series No. 91).

Chapter 7: THE ROOTS OF LIBERATION

1. Herbert J. Muller, *Issues of Freedom* (New York: Harper and Brothers, 1960), p. 40.
2. John H. Hallowell, *The Moral Foundation of Democracy* (Chicago: University of Chicago Press, 1954), p. 79.
3. Adam Schaff, *A Philosophy of Man* (New York: Dell Publishing Co. Inc., 1963), p. 110.
4. Ibid.
5. John Erskine, *The Human Life of Jesus* (New York: Wm. Morrow & Co., 1945), pp. 197-198.

6. Paul L. Maier, "Sejanus, Pilate and The Date of The Crucifixion," *Church History*, 37 (March 1968), p. 11.
7. Ibid, pp. 11-12.
8. Roger Garaudy, "Faith and Revolution," *Ecumenical Review*, 25 (January 1973), p. 69.
9. Ibid.
10. Ibid.

CONCLUSION

1. Matthew Arnold, *Culture and Anarchy*. Vol. 5 of *The Complete Prose Works of Matthew Arnold*, R. H. Super, ed., (Ann Arbor: University of Michigan Press, 1965), p. 106.
2. Gordon George Lord Byron, "The Prisoner of Chillon," in *British Poetry and Prose*, P. R. Lieder et al, ed., 3rd ed. (Boston: Houghton Mifflin, 1950), 2:145.
3. Franz Boas, "Liberty Among Primitive People in *Freedom: Its Meaning*, Ruth Nandi Anshen, ed. (N.Y.: Harcourt Brace & Co., 1940), p. 376.
4. Bruce Stokes, "Worker-Owned Businesses Work," *The Nation*, Feb. 17, 1979.
5. Ibid.
6. Walter Brueggeman, *The Prophetic Imagination* (Philadelphia: Fortress Press, 1978), p. 96.

INDEX

DATE DUE

HIGHSMITH 45-220

104837